THE DOCTOR AND NEGLIGENCE

BY THE SAME AUTHOR

The Doctor and The Law

THE DOCTOR AND NEGLIGENCE

J Leahy Taylor MB, BS, DMJ, MRCGP

Deputy Secretary,
The Medical Protection Society Limited London

WITH A FOREWORD BY

F Harwood Stevenson

Chairman of the Council of
the Medical Protection Society

Pitman Medical

First published 1971

SIR ISAAC PITMAN AND SONS LTD
Pitman House, Parker Street, Kingsway, London, WC2B 5PB
P.O. Box 6038, Portal Street, Nairobi, Kenya

SIR ISAAC PITMAN (AUST.) PTY. LTD
Pitman House, 158 Bouverie Street, Carlton, Victoria 3053, Australia

PITMAN PUBLISHING COMPANY S.A. LTD
P.O. Box 11231, Johannesburg, South Africa

PITMAN PUBLISHING CORPORATION
6 East 43rd Street, New York, N.Y. 10017, U.S.A.

SIR ISAAC PITMAN (CANADA) LTD
495 Wellington Street West, Toronto 135, Canada

THE COPP CLARK PUBLISHING COMPANY
517 Wellington Street West, Toronto 135, Canada

ISBN: 0 272 76060 9

Printed by photo-lithography and made in Great Britain at the Pitman Press, Bath.
01 3602 81

Foreword

Dr Leahy Taylor, in his new book, makes clear for us the legal concepts of negligence as the Law sees it in our professional context. He also traces the developments in the Courts which have brought us to where we stand in 1971. Finally, he ventures to explore some possible extensions of the Law that time might bring.

An experienced general medical practitioner before becoming Deputy Secretary of The Medical Protection Society, he brings an informed sympathy and understanding to the illustrative histories, carefully classified, which he quotes from the Society's records. But, chosen as they are as examples of unfortunate incidents, the crux of the matter must be recognised; that in many instances they were in fact avoidable.

One is impressed by Dr Leahy Taylor's clarity of demonstration and argument, and the care with which he has constructed each section of the book. It fills, with all the relevant information, a space that has too long existed on our shelves. Any student or doctor having read it must be better equipped to fulfil his duties to his patients, and consequently to protect, and indeed enhance, both his own reputation and that of our profession.

I was delighted when he told me of his intention, and having seen the script am sure that his work will be read both widely and thoughtfully.

F. HARWOOD STEVENSON

Preface

My old and much-respected teacher of forensic medicine used to tell his class that provided they retained that knowledge which they possessed at the time of their qualification and acted upon it, they were safe from any action in negligence.

Would that the same could be said today. The facts, however, are very different. The Court expects, and indeed demands that the doctor will keep abreast of such knowledge as is generally known to practitioners of his standing and experience, and that he will at all times and under all circumstances employ that knowledge with adequate skill and care.

To maintain this standard in the clinical field amid the flood of new knowledge and the pressure of day-to-day work is no light task. But added to this is the necessity of keeping some contact with the equally rapidly developing medico-legal field. New methods of investigation and treatment give rise to new problems of the required standard of skill and care. Enthusiasm must not outrun discretion. Familiarity with certain situations that have never in the past caused trouble must not be allowed to tempt one to cut corners and take chances. It is necessary to remind oneself constantly that it is the patient who is in fact the chance taker.

This book will I hope provide doctors and medical students with an understanding of the dangers they face in practice today, for, for both them and their patients, prophylaxis is preferable to therapy.

The cases referred to are largely drawn from the files of the Medical Protection Society and for this facility I am greatly indebted to the President and Council of the Society. My thanks go also to Mr W. G. Hawkins, Solicitor to the Society, who has made a number of most helpful suggestions regarding the text, to Dr F. Harwood Stevenson, Chairman of Council of the Society, for his Foreword, and to my secretary, Mrs G. Roberts, without whose help these pages would never have seen the light of day.

May the perusal of this text lead at least one reader at some time in his life to have second thoughts that may cause him to take some step that protects his patients' health, his own reputation, and the funds of his protection society.

J.L.T.

Contents

1. The Legal Concept of Negligence

Negligence is a legal, not a medical, concept. This simple fact should hearten, but will probably dismay, doctors who find themselves confronted with an allegation of negligence. It should hearten them because a finding of negligence in a civil court, or a decision to settle rather than contest a claim in negligence, does not necessarily imply any condemnation by their professional colleagues. It implies at most an actual or an anticipated finding by a judge – a layman in matters medical – that on the evidence presented to him their handling of the case did not come up to the standard required by the law. It is no disrespect to Her Majesty's judges to consider that their condemnation should disturb a doctor less than condemnation by his professional brethren.

There are many reasons why this should be so. Judges would be more –or less – than human if they did not allow the disfigured child, the young widow, or the disabled workman the benefit of any doubt that remained after experts on both sides had had their say. The sympathy of the court is a far from negligible factor which the defendant's advisers must weigh with care before deciding to proceed. Not only is it far from negligible; it is also far from constant. When, shortly before trial, a conference with Counsel is held, the question of which Judge will likely take the case can be a very material consideration. 'I am sorry to have to tell you that Mr Justice X is ill and we are likely to come before Mr Justice Y' can lead to a detailed reappraisal of the prospects of success. Then there is the gift of hindsight – retrospective medicine is the simplest of all specialties and has many devotees; indeed it can be difficult in the extreme to divest entirely one's mind of the knowledge of what came after and to report objectively on the position as it was at the relevant time. The sequence of events leading step by step to the tragedy as expounded with great care and skill by learned

Counsel can hardly fail to carry the message of causation linkage, and foreseeability. The ease of this line of reasoning is heightened by the essential difference between the legal and medical approach to a problem. To the lawyer precedence and logic must, if followed with due diligence, lead to the correct result. To the doctor, while the main path of approach is founded on physiological concepts, which if not accepted as the whole truth have at least stood some test of time, his final decision must also take into account his personal experience, the weight he personally gives to the opinions of others, and his assessment of the patient and not just of the disease. When a wrong choice is made, how easy for law to criticise and condemn; how difficult for medicine to explain and excuse.

Again, while the writer has every admiration for the skill with which the legally trained mind assimilates matters medical, the Judge's view must be less than complete. It is impossible to convey precisely how the matter appeared to this particular doctor with his particular experience and having regard to the other duties and responsibilities with which he was concerned at the particular time. 'Time' can indeed be all important, and can anyone without personal experience appreciate and evaluate what is and what is not reasonable under the conditions of present-day medical practice?

The fact that negligence is a legal and not a medical concept will, however, dismay rather than encourage the doctor, because so often he is fully prepared to justify his actions to his peers whose opinions he respects, and whom he knows can put themselves in his place. He is therefore not a little put out when it is explained to him that it is through legal rather than medical eyes that the matter must be viewed. To explain to a doctor that a case is better settled when at the same time one must admit that the vast majority of doctors would have acted precisely as did he can be an unrewarding task. All such can then take heart in that the estimate of the Judge's views is based purely on precedence and experience, and that in all but a small minority of cases the view of the doctor's professional colleagues is that of sympathy rather than criticism. It can also be thought that a Judge, finding a doctor negligent, when he has done what most of his colleagues would have done, is in effect paying a compliment – a somewhat backhanded one perhaps – to the high standard expected of and maintained by the medical profession.

In spite of the fact that negligence is a legal and not a medical concept, in general its proof requires, when the defendant is a medical man, medical witnesses prepared to testify before the court. One at times hears complaints of difficulties lawyers have encountered in securing the services of expert witnesses in such cases. In countries where lawyers work on a contingency fee basis such a difficulty is quite understandable, for only by the medical profession declining to co-operate can the activities of the ambulance-chasing lawyer be curbed. In the United Kingdom difficulty should seldom arise; the last such complaint that came to the author's notice concerned a small town lawyer whose reputation for undertaking speculative actions had it seemed necessitated his seeking his witnesses over an ever-increasing radius.

Certainly there is no 'conspiracy of silence' in the profession. The three societies that advise the medical and dental profession in legal matters all stress that there is a public duty on all those possessing expert knowledge to assist the furtherance of justice. Their members are then encouraged to assist by giving their testimony and are assured that, provided they do not appear in this role with undue frequency, they will not meet with criticism within their own profession. There is, then, no objection or difficulty on the theoretical level. When it comes to the practical expression it is, regrettably, a not uncommon result that the frustrated expert whose time has been treated in a somewhat cavalier manner by the court decides he has no taste for further medico-legal work. The cure for this condition does not lie with the physician.

Definition

Negligence is a tort, i.e. a civil wrong, that consists of a breach of a duty to use reasonable skill and care, resulting in damage. The four Ds are the essentials of negligence: there must have been a Duty, a Dereliction of that Duty, Direct causation and Damage.

Regarding a doctor's duty, there can seldom be any doubt of his moral and professional duty. Regarding his legal duty, the position is not so clear. Certainly he has no legal duty to assist at an accident and if he does so he is, of course, liable should he be negligent in the care he gives or the skill he displays. There is nothing at all unreasonable about this; a medical student, a first-aid worker or a totally unskilled member of the public would be in precisely the same position except that the standard of skill and care required by the law would differ. Once, however, a doctor has accepted a patient for treatment of a particular condition, he has a legal duty to use reasonable skill and care until the patient no longer requires, or no longer desires further attendance.

General practitioners in the National Health Service are obliged by their Terms of Service to treat certain categories of persons such as patients on their list and patients who have met with an accident or other emergency. This does not, of course, prohibit a patient on the National Health Service list of a certain doctor from attending another doctor, nor the second doctor accepting the patient for treatment provided he ascertains that the patient is not already under treatment for that condition.

The question occasionally arises as to whether a National Health Service doctor is bound to continue treating a patient whose conduct has led the doctors and the hospital authority concerned to wish to terminate the patient's attendance. In a recent unreported case, *The Royal London Homeopathic Hospital Management Committee* v. *Thorne,* the court stated that there was no such obligation upon the hospital or the doctors employed therein.

In general, however, once a doctor undertakes the care of a patient, he assumes a duty towards him and it matters not whether the patient is private, National Health Service, or indeed is being treated entirely gratuitously. Questions can occasionally arise as to liability in respect of advice given. Doctors would certainly be wise not to give offhand advice but much would depend upon the precise circumstances, and the court would in all probability consider whether, in the giving of the advice, there was an intention to assume responsibility by the doctor and an intention to act on the advice received by the plaintiff. Social life for the doctor would become quite impossible if every word he uttered on a medical topic to a layman could make him liable in negligence.

A recent case, *Buckle* v. *de Launay*,[1] concerned a circumstance in which the doctor had a clear duty to give advice. Dr de Launay prescribed tranylcypromine, and two days later Mrs Buckle ate cheese which after a further two days resulted in her death from a brain haemorrhage. The crucial question before the court was whether adequate advice had been given regarding the eating of foods with a high tyramine content. In the event, the court was satisfied that Dr de Launay had prohibited the eating of cheese, but doctors would be well advised to have some written evidence of the advice given in such cases.

Dereliction of the duty assumed is the nub of negligence. To this point is directed the bulk of the argument in court, and here the testimony of expert witnesses is crucial. Certainly the court can find a doctor negligent without expert witnesses – judgment belongs to the court, not to the medical profession – but it is, on the whole, unlikely to do so. Indeed, as one cannot imagine the defendant doctor being without expert testimony, it is evident that the court would be extremely hesitant to find for a plaintiff who was not likewise provided. Reasonable as it is for the court to prefer one expert's view to another, it is *prima facie* unreasonable to reject the evidence of the only expert called.

Direct causation can pose thorny questions. If a doctor fails to take an X-ray, thereby failing to diagnose a fracture, and if it be agreed that the failure was negligent, then the extra pain and suffering, the extra loss of wages, and the extra resultant disability caused by that failure have all resulted directly from the doctor's negligence, and the court will award appropriate damages. But what of the promotion the patient might have had, had he returned to work earlier? What of the extra expenses of the household owing to the patient being unable to drive a car, undertake house repairs, mow the lawn, and so on. What of the patient's wife's loss of wages when she stayed at home to look after him, and the resultant inability to pay for the children's extra tuition in subjects in which they showed the greatest promise? It would indeed be strange if all that were claimed were true; how many budding Beethovens have been cut off in their prime owing to someone's negligent treatment of their injured finger or to the financial stringency resulting from the negligent manner in which their injured parent was dealt with? Margate may be fine

1. *The Times*, 7th and 8th July 1970.

for the annual holiday but convalescence following an injury due to another's negligence requires, nay demands, a sojourn in the south of France. One claim, submitted in all seriousness by a solicitor, included a not inconsiderable sum for extra cigarettes necessitated by the insomnia resulting from the pain caused by the alleged negligent treatment.

To these flights of fancy – or gestures of greed – the law has two answers. First, the chain of consequences is brought to an abrupt halt by a *novus actus interveniens.* Once some fresh incident occurs which materially affects the patient's progress or resultant disability, the defendant doctor's liability is at an end. This may be a further accident, an inter current illness, an unreasonable decision not to accept further treatment, or extraneous factors affecting the patient's salary, etc. In the Oropesa[2] case Lord Justice Wright said, 'It must always be shown that there is something which I will call ultroneous, something unwarrantable, a new cause coming in, disturbing the sequence of events, something that can be described as either unreasonable or extraneous or extrinsic'.

Second, the remoteness of the alleged loss: this can be difficult to define, but in any case the point comes where the court will determine that subsequent losses are too remote from the original to give rise to liability. Remoteness is not in general to be equated with foreseeability, and the negligent doctor may expect to be held responsible for the results of his negligent act, not only for those results he did or should have foreseen. Consequences are, however, unending, and it is the court's discretion to determine at what point they become too remote to qualify.

There is, however, one important decision that may give an adequate defence in certain, as yet not completely defined, cases. This was the 'Wagon Mound'[3] case, where an extraordinary sequence of events took place. Furnace oil from the defendant's ship drifted towards the plaintiff's wharf, where molten metal falling on cotton waste ignited the oil. Lord Simmons said: 'The essential factor in determining liability is whether the damage is of such a kind as the reasonable man should have foreseen', and 'It does not seem consonant with current ideas of justice or morality that for an act of negligence, however slight or venial,

2. (1943) The Oropesa, 1, All E.R. 211.

3. *Overseas Tank Ship* v. *Morts Docks.* 1.All E.R. 404. 2WLR. 126. PC.

which results in some trivial forseeable damage, the actor should be liable for all consequences, however unforeseeable and however grave, so long as they can be said to be direct'.

Damage, the fourth D, must be proved before damages, the financial solaceum, will be awarded by the court. The use of this one word in singular and plural form to imply such differing aspects of the subject is unfortunate, and a word will be said about each in turn. The onus is on the plaintiff to show that he incurred actual, not potential, damage as a direct consequence of the defendant's failure to use reasonable skill and care. This is not in general a difficult hurdle. Delay in diagnosis will almost inevitably be accepted as causing increased pain and suffering. The swab remaining in the vagina for a few days after the episiotomy is sutured will, beyond peradventure, cause symptoms that bear little or no relationship to those of the patient who has overlooked a tampon for some months. What can be difficult, however, is to determine whether, and if so to what extent, the final result is worsened by the delay, and it is common for plaintiffs and their legal advisers to proceed on the wholly incorrect assumption that with adequate medical care there would have been no residual disability. Having then assessed the damage caused, translated it into financial terms in the light of previously decided cases, and added to this any loss or disbursements arising from the negligence, the plaintiff's legal advisers are in a position to quantify the damages claimed.

Damages awarded by the court have as their objective not, save in exceptional circumstances, the punishment of the tortfeasor but the placing of the plaintiff, so far as money can do so, in the same position as he would have been had it not been for the defendant's negligence. It follows that the degree of negligence is immaterial in the civil courts; what matters is what if anything, the plaintiff suffered from the negligence. This fact has results that may appear illogical at first sight. It is usually cheaper to kill than to maim and it is, in general, more expensive to be negligent to one's wealthy patients than to those in more humble circumstances.

Damages awarded will then take into account financial loss, present and future, expenses present and future, pain and suffering, loss of the amenities of life and loss of expectation of life. In assessing the damages to be paid where the breadwinner has lost his life, regard must be had to his age, his income, the number of years he would, without the negligence, have been expected to maintain that income, and the amount of that income normally spent upon himself. Where, instead of losing his life, he has been rendered incapable of earning, the extra cost of caring for him must also be considered. In this regard the plaintiff is entitled to make use of private medical facilities and it cannot be objected that he could have saved expense by use of the National Health Service. This last fact is an exception to the general rule that a plaintiff must take reasonable steps to mitigate his loss. What is in any particular case reasonable is for the court to determine. The defendant cannot demand that the plaintiff act with perfect knowledge or ideal wisdom but should he unreasonably refuse treatment or act in a way that a reasonable man would expect to aggravate his injuries, the court will reduce the damages by the appropriate amount.

Where life has been lost the claim on behalf of the relatives is made under the Fatal Accidents Acts (1846-1959) and takes account of the amount of their dependancy as outlined above. Loss of expectation of life – a claim on behalf of the estate – is pursued under the Law Reform (Miscellaneous Provisions) Act, 1934, and the normal maximum awarded under this head is £500. It will be apparent that the same act of negligence may give rise to damages ranging from, in the case of a man without dependants, a few hundred pounds, to, in the case of a man earning a high salary and with a large family, such sum as will maintain that family in the state to which they have been accustomed for so long as the breadwinner would have been expected to provide for them.

The damages so far discussed have been 'general' damages which are those awarded for pain, suffering, loss of amenities of life etc. and 'special' damages which are those relating to actual losses and expenses incurred as a result of the negligence. In the vast majority of cases these are the only two types of damages with which a court is concerned, but occasionally exceptional considerations arise. Where the breach is purely technical and no real harm has resulted 'nominal' damages may be awarded, and where the court feel that, although the plaintiff has succeeded, the case should never have been brought, then 'contemptuous' damages may mark the court's disapproval. At the other extreme 'aggravated' damages may be awarded where the defendant's act or omission was performed with some improper motive. 'Exemplary' damages are most unlikely to be awarded in any case relating to medical negligence, and perhaps this could occur only were it shown that the negligent act was performed wilfully and with the object of personal profit. It is somewhat illogical that in the case of 'aggravated' and 'exemplary' damages the plaintiff obtains something more than the case is apparently worth as a result of the civil court taking unto itself the right to inflict punishment.

Before leaving the subject of damages, contributory negligence and joint negligence must be mentioned. Cases occasionally arise where the patient's own negligence contributes towards the injury. The patient, other than a child, who meddles with equipment, takes a meal shortly before an anaesthetic though specially instructed otherwise, or, a medicine having been incorrectly dispensed, takes double the dose stated on the label, can hardly expect to blame the whole of his misfortunes on his medical adviser. In such cases the court will, having assessed the damages on the basis of full liability, deduct such proportion as appears appropriate in view of the plaintiff's degree of blameworthiness. Joint negligence occurs when two or more persons other than the plaintiff himself have been negligent. The plaintiff is entitled to sue any one of those responsible for the total amount of loss and damage suffered. By the terms of the Law Reform (Married Women and Tortfeasors) Act, 1935, any tortfeasor so sued is enabled to claim an appropriate contribution from any other tortfeasor who shared liability towards the plaintiff in respect of the same damage.

Liability

Once satisfied that his client has a claim in negligence, the plaintiff's solicitor's next task is to consider against whom the claim should be made – to determine, in fact, where lies the liability.

The first consideration is that an adult is responsible for his own acts or omissions. The patient could then proceed against the nurse employed in hospital or general practice in respect of her own negligence. He is unlikely to do so because of the dictum *respondeat superior* which places a vicarious liability upon an employer in respect of the negligence of his employee in the performance of the duties of his employment and therefore, where a nurse is involved, the hospital management committee or the general practitioner employer is likely to be cited as defendant.

Where doctors are concerned different considerations apply. Where a general practitioner is alleged to have been negligent, he alone or the partnership of which he is a member or to which he is an assistant may be sued. It is therefore imperative that before a general practitioner takes on a new partner or assistant he satisfies himself that the newcomer is adequately covered against any action that might be taken against the partnership. Such cover is, of course, usually obtained by membership of one of the medical protection associations. Where a doctor in hospital practice is involved, he himself, his employing authority, or both, may be cited. Should the hospital authority be found negligent in respect of the doctor's acts, then in strict law, action could be taken against the doctor with a view to obtaining reimbursement. It is, however, only too evident that were relationships of this nature to exist between hospital authority and hospital doctor, the patients would inevitably be the losers and, to avoid such situations arising, the conduct of these cases is governed by an agreement between the Department of Health and the protection organisations.

This agreement provides; first, that either party to the agreement may at any time decide to settle an action assuming full liability for damages, each party paying its own costs; second, that where both parties agree to explore a settlement this should be sought in such proportions as they may agree, and if agreement, cannot be reached, then in equal shares; third, where an action proceeds into court, the parties should endeavour to reach agreement as to the shares in which an adverse verdict will be met. Failing agreement before trial a further attempt to agree should be made following the trial. Should agreement prove impossible, the damages and costs awarded to the plaintiff should be divided in equal shares among those found liable.

Standard of Care

The standard required of the doctor is that reasonably to be expected of a practitioner of the same status, experience and qualifications working under the same conditions. The position was succinctly stated by Lord Chief Justice Goddard in these terms: 'Anybody may feel a sense of grievance who is injured by an accident but . . . . people are far too apt to think that because an accident happens therefore it must be due to negligence . . . . Any person who submits himself to . . . . any form of surgical operation is voluntarily submitting himself to a risk. If the injury is brought about by a disregard of ordinary professional skill and competence, why then he is entitled to recover damages against the practitioner but if there is not, the mere fact that he happened to sustain an injury during the course of the operation to which he submitted himself gives him no cause of complaint or action against the practitioner. No practitioner is an insurer that no accident will happen'.

What is reasonable in any given case will likely be decided by the court in the light of the expert evidence put before it. Herein lies one particular difficulty for the defence, for their expert will likely be asked in cross-examination whether the same tragic result might have occurred had he been conducting the patient's treatment, and it is a man of unusual qualities who will unhesitatingly and without reservation admit that a similar result would have been likely.

The experts, of course, may disagree, and while the court is entitled to prefer one expert opinion to another, in general, negligence will not be found to have occurred where it is shown that there is a responsible body of opinion within the profession that supports the action taken by the defendant. This, of course, poses problems for the doctor whose patient meets with misfortune when undergoing a new procedure, especially when there exists a reasonably satisfactory line of treatment for the patient's complaint. It is obvious that it can be negligent to employ methods that recent advances have rendered out of date but the practitioner who is in advance of his contemporaries may be in no better position. The question was considered by Lord Clyde in a Scottish case, *Hunter* v. *Hanley*[4]: 'A deviation is not neccessarily evidence of negligence. Indeed it would be disastrous if this were so, for all inducement to progress in medical science would be destroyed. Even a substantial deviation from normal practice may be warranted by the particular circumstances. In the realm of diagnosis and treatment there is ample scope for genuine difference of opinion and one man is clearly not negligent merely because his conclusion differs from that of other professional men or because he has displayed less skill and

4. (1955) *Hunter* v. *Hanley* SC200.

knowledge than others would have shown . . . . To establish liability by a doctor where deviation from normal practice is alleged three facts must first be established. First of all it must be proved there is a usual and normal practice. Secondly, it must be proved that the doctor has not adopted that practice, and thirdly (this is of crucial importance) it must be established that the course the doctor adopted is one that no professional man of ordinary skill would have taken if he had been acting with ordinary care.'

So much for the general standard of care, but what of the practitioner who professes specialist skills? The patient is clearly entitled to expect in such a case to have the benefit of those skills. When the practitioner holds a consultant post, then within the confines of his specialty a high degree of skill can be required; outside them, e.g. a pathologist called to deal with an emergency obstetric situation, a much lower standard may be accepted. The essential, however, is not the position the practioner holds but what he leads his patient to believe. If the practitioner conveys to his patient that he has special training, skill, experience or qualification in the matter in which he is consulted, then he must expect to be judged by the standards he has set himself. The patient can – and most assuredly will – very reasonably claim that it was the fact of the practitioner's particular knowledge that induced him to consent to the treatment proposed.

Before leaving this topic it should be mentioned that the possession of special knowledge and skill can be conveyed in different ways. A plate in Harley Street suggests to many laymen an above-average standard of competence and, perhaps more important, the fee that customarily goes with it, may well convey the same impression to a Judge. The fee is, however, but a single factor indicative of the standard of care the patient can reasonably require, and more than one practitioner of the very highest standard has found that where he has given gratuitous treatment to one he thought his friend, an allegation of negligence has followed. If a specialist register were to be created in this country, as has been done in certain others, the standard of skill and care required in any case might become that much the more certain.

The general practitioner in the National Health Service has, as one of his terms of service, a requirement to render to his patients 'all proper and necessary treatment'. While there is a world of difference between the Service Committee, which considers whether the doctor has complied with this item of his terms of service, and the High or County Court, which considers an action in negligence, nevertheless the Service Committee procedure has been grossly abused as a free trial run to test the prospects of success in legal proceedings.

Res Ipsa Loquitur

In general, the onus of proof is upon he who affirms, i.e. it is for the plaintiff to prove that his damage or loss results from the negligence of the defendant, and further it is for the plaintiff to state in what precise particulars the defendant failed to use reasonable skill and care. This can be a heavy burden to discharge, especially where a number of persons have had a hand in the patient's treatment and where the treatment has been of such a complexity that the plaintiff can at best have but an imperfect knowledge of it. Cases do arise where the onus passes to the defendant; these are cases where the result itself implies negligence and the court accepts that the maxim, *res ipsa loquitur* – the thing speaks for itself – applies. One such case was that of *Cassidy* v. *Ministry of Health*[5]. Here the patient underwent an operation for Dupuytren's contracture affecting two fingers. Following postoperative splinting for some fourteen days, not only were the two affected fingers still bent and stiff but two other fingers were also affected. The Court of Appeal, in reversing the decision of the trial court, considered it to be a case of *res ipsa loquitur*, and Lord Justice Denning said: 'If the plaintiff had to prove that some particular doctor or nurse was negligent he would not be able to do it. But he was not put to that impossible task; he says: "I went into the hospital to be cured of two stiff fingers. I have come out with four stiff fingers and my hand is useless. That should not have happened if due care had been used. Explain it if you can".'

The maxim is particularly useful to the plaintiff where, by the very nature of things, he cannot know whose error led to his being harmed. That which has occurred while the patient was under an anaesthetic, e.g. a retained instrument or swab, or a burn discovered on recovering consciousness, would probably be

5. 1951 2KB 343.

held to make the maxim applicable. This point was referred to in the case of *Roe* v. *Ministry of Health*[6] by Lord Justice Denning in these terms: 'I do not think that the hospital authorities and Dr Graham (the anaesthetist) can both avoid giving an explanation by the simple expedient of each throwing the responsibility on to the other. If an injured person shows that one or other or both of two persons injure him but cannot say which of them it was, then he is not defeated altogether. He can call on each of them for an explanation.'

6. (1954) 1.WLR. 128 (1954) 2QB. 71.

2. Leading Cases in Medical Negligence

This chapter proposes to take a chronological look at the manner in which case law in negligence has developed. The importance of this view stems, of course, from the legal concept of precedence. Decisions of the House of Lords do not bind the House itself but are binding upon lower courts. Those of the Court of Appeal bind the High Court and those of the High Court bind the County Court. Decisions of other similar jurisdictions while carrying no precedent, may nevertheless have persuasive authority. If any decisions appear not to follow precedent, this is because the court has felt able to distinguish between the cases and has therefore not felt bound to follow the previous decision.

With this brief introduction the cases will now speak for themselves.

1838: *Lanphier* v. *Phipos*[1]

Chief Justice Tindal said:

> 'Every person who enters into a learned profession undertakes to bring to the exercise of it a reasonable degree of care and skill. He does not undertake, if he is an attorney, that at all events you shall gain your case, nor does a surgeon undertake that he will perform a cure, nor does he undertake to use the highest degree of skill. There may be persons who have higher education and greater advantages than he has but he undertakes to bring a fair, reasonable and competent degree of skill.'

1860: *Ritchey* v. *West*[2]

This case was noteworthy as the only medical malpractice case in which Abraham Lincoln appeared as Counsel. Keziah West

1. 8 C & P. 475.
2. Supreme Court of Illinois. Case No. 23. Ill.385.

sued Dr Ritchey in respect of his treatment of the plaintiff's fracture dislocation of the wrist, alleging that the splintage was inadequate and that Dr Ritchey did not attend on the following day as he had agreed. The Circuit Court found for the plaintiff and Dr Ritchey appealed. Lincoln appealed for Ritchey, and the Supreme Court upheld the decision of the Circuit Court, stating:

> 'There was a want of ordinary care or skill or both manifested in the treatment of the case.'

And further,

> 'Had he returned, as his duty and his agreement required, in all probability the visit would have resulted in detecting the true situation of the injury and relief might then have been obtained by the employment of the necessary surgical aid.'

1862: *Rich* v. *Pierpont*[3]

This case established the point that a practitioner is not liable merely because some other practitioner might have shown greater skill and knowledge.

1909: *Hillyer* v. *St. Bartholomew's Hospital*[4]

Lord Justice Farwell said:

> '. . . All professional men (are) employed by the defendants to exercise their profession to the best of their abilities according to their own discretion; but in exercising it they are in no way under the orders or bound to obey the directions of the defendants.'

This view was, however, modified in *Gold* v. *Essex County Council* – *vide infra,* p 19.

1914: *Mitchell* v. *Dixon;* a South African case[5]

> 'The mere fact that the accident occurred was not in itself prima facie proof of negligence because the needle might have been fractured by causes beyond the control of the operator – by the movements of the patient, for example. So that the maxim *res ipsa loquitur* could have no application,'

and in the same case:

> 'No human being is infallible; and in the present state of science even the most eminent specialist may be at fault in detecting the true nature of a diseased condition. A practitioner

3. 3 F.& F. 35. 4. (1909) 2KB. 820. 5. (1914) App. D. 519.

can only be held liable . . . if his mistake is of such a nature as to imply an absence of reasonable skill and care on his part, regard being had to the ordinary level of skill in the profession.'

1924: *Van Wyk* v. *Lewis*[6] – *a South African case*

"In deciding what is reasonable the court will have regard to the general level of skill and diligence possessed and exercised at the time by members of the branch of the profession to which the practitioner belongs. The evidence of qualified surgeons or physicians is of the greatest assistance in estimating that general level. And their evidence may well be influenced by local experience; but I desire to guard myself from assenting to the principle approved in some American decisions that the standard of skill which should be exercised is that which presides in the particular locality where the practitioner happens to reside. The ordinary medical practitioner should, as it seems to me, exercise the same degree of skill and care whether he carries on his work in the town or the country, in one place or another. The fact that several incompetent or careless practitioners happen to settle at the same place cannot affect the standard of diligence and skill which local patients have a right to expect.'

1925: *Rex* v. *Bateman*[7]

'. . . It is no doubt conceivable that a qualified man may be held liable for recklessly undertaking a case which he knew, or should have known, to be beyond his powers, or for making his patient the subject of reckless experiment.'

1930: *Bank of Montreal* v. *Dominion Gresham Guarantee and Casualty Company*[8]

'Neglect of duty does not cease by repetition to be neglect of duty.'

1932: *Donoghue* v. *Stevenson*[9]
Lord MacMillan:

'The categories of negligence are never closed.'

6. (1924) App. D.438.
7. (1925) 94. LJ. KB791.
8. (1930) AC 659.
9. (1932) AC 562, 639.

1934: *Vancouver General Hospital* v. *McDaniel*[10]

> 'A defendant charged with negligence can clear his feet if he shows that he has acted in accord with general and approved practice.'

1935: *Daniels* v. *Heskin – an Irish case*[11]

A needle broke while the perineum was being repaired, and the doctor informed the midwife but did not inform the patient or her husband. Judgment was given for the practitioner, and in dismissing the subsequent appeal, Lavery J. said:

> 'It is clear that there are some matters which a doctor must disclose in order to afford his patient an opportunity of deciding whether she accepted his view or wished to consult another doctor, and an opportunity to make a choice between alternative courses . . . . . On the other hand there are matters which the doctor must decide for himself having accepted the responsibility of treating his patient and having regard to his professional skill and knowledge on which she relied.'

Regarding the decision not to inform the patient the Judge said:

> 'That was a reasonable decision. It is not necessary to show that it was the right decision.'

In the same case Kingsmill J. said:

> 'I cannot admit any abstract duty to tell patients what is the matter with them or to particularise, to say that a needle has been left in their tissues. All depends on the circumstances . . . I do not wish to suggest that a doctor would always be justified in keeping such knowledge to himself.'

1935: *Marshall* v. *Lindsey County Council*[12]

> '. . . What is reasonable in a world not wholly composed of wise men and women must depend on what people presumed to be reasonable constantly do.'

1939: *Mahon* v. *Osborne*[13]

> 'The standard of care the law requires is not insurance against accidental slips. It is such a degree of care as a normally skilful member of the profession may reasonably be expected to

10. (1934) 152 LT.56.
11. (1935) 1LT.189.
12. (1935) 1KB.516.
13. (1939) 1 A11 ER. 535 2KB14.

> exercise in the actual circumstances of the case in question. It is not every slip or mistake which imports negligence,'

and

> 'As it is the task of the surgeon to put the swabs in, so it is his task to take them out . . . unless there be evidence that the nature of the case be such that no search of any description – be it by eye, finger or mechanical means – was possible, a surgeon cannot show that he used reasonable care . . . by saying 'I relied on the nurse's count', and further 'While, to omit the precautions afforded by a count might well be negligent, it does not follow that he fully discharges his duty by merely asking and being told that the count is right.'

1942: *Gold* v. *Essex County Council*[14]

Lord Greene:

> 'The true ground on which the hospital escapes liability for the act of a nurse who, whether in the operating theatre or elsewhere, is acting under the instructions of the surgeon or doctor, is not that *pro hac vice* she ceases to be the servant of the hospital but that she is not guilty of negligence if she carries out the orders of the surgeon however negligent those orders may be. I can see no reason or principle why, if she negligently carries out an order, the hospital shall not be liable.'

Lord Goddard added –

> 'If a doctor, in a moment of carelessness, perhaps by the use of a wrong symbol in a prescription, ordered a dose which, to an experienced ward sister, was obviously incorrect and dangerous, I think it might well be held to be negligence if she administered it without obtaining confirmation from the doctor or higher authority. In the stress of an operation, however, I suppose that the first thing required of a nurse would be an unhesitating obedience to the orders of the surgeon.'

From the same case came Lord Greene's explanation of the duty owed by a hospital:

> 'The person accused of a breach of the obligation cannot escape liability because he employed another person, whether a servant or agent, to discharge it on his behalf, and this is

14. (1942) A11 ER. 237 (1942) 2KB 293.

> equally true whether or not the obligation involves the use of skill. It is also true that if the obligation is undertaken by a corporation or a body of trustees or governors, they cannot escape liability for its breach any more than can an individual, and it is no answer to say that the obligation is one which on the face of it they could never perform themselves. Nor can it make any difference that the obligation is assumed gratuitously by a person, body or corporation which does not act for profit.'

1949: *Murrin* v. *Jones – a Canadian case*[15]

This case upheld the principle that a practitioner need not warn his patient against the obvious – negligence was alleged in failure to warn a patient who had all his teeth extracted of the danger of serious haemorrhage.

1950: *Clarke* v. *Adams*[16]

Short wave diathermy was administered with the warning:

> 'When I turn on the machine I want you to experience a comfortable warmth and nothing more; if you do I want you to tell me.'

The patient was burned and succeeded in the action on the grounds that the warning did not sufficiently stress the danger.

1951: *Wood* v. *Thurston*[17]

A casualty officer misled by a patient's dull reaction to pain due to alcohol, failed to use a stethescope and failed to diagnose, *inter alia,* eighteen fractured ribs. The patient died, and the casualty officer was found to have been negligent.

1951: *Cassidy* v. *Ministry of Health*[18]

Lord Denning's pronouncement was one of prime importance in the development of negligence. Speaking of the liability of hospitals he said:

> 'Clearly if he is a paying patient, paying them directly for their treatment of him, they must take reasonable care of him, and why should it make any difference if he does not pay them directly but only indirectly through the rates which he pays

15. (1949) DLR.403. 16. (1950) 94 S.Jo.599.
17. (1951) CLY 2361; (1951) *The Times,* 25th May.
18. (1951) 1 A11 ER 574(CA); (1951) 2KB 343.

to the local authority or through insurance contributions which he makes in order to get the treatment? I see no difference at all. Even if he is so poor that he can pay nothing and the hospital treats him out of charity, still the hospital authorities are under a duty to take reasonable care of him . . . The hospital authorities cannot, of course, do it by themselves; they have no ears to listen through the stethescope and no hands to hold the surgeon's knife. They must do it by the staff which they employ. And if their staff are negligent in giving the treatment, they are just as liable for that negligence as is anyone else who employs others to do his duties for him . . . Who employs the doctor or surgeon – is it the patient or the hospital authorities? If the patient himself selects and employs the doctor or surgeon as in Hillyer's case, the hospital authorities are, of course, not liable for his negligence because he is not employed by them. But where the doctor or surgeon, be he consultant or not, is employed and paid not by the patient but by the hospital authorities, I am of the opinion that the hospital authorities are liable for his negligence in treating the patient. It does not depend upon whether the contract under which he was employed was a contract of service or a contract for services . . . Where a person is himself under a duty to use care he cannot get rid of his responsibility by delegating the performance of it to someone else, no matter whether the delegation be to a servant under a contract of service or to an independent contractor under a contract for services.'

1952: *Jones* v. *Manchester Corporation*[19]
The employing authority sought to obtain complete indemnity from the employee doctor. The Court of Appeal held that an employer is not entitled to indemnity from an employee if he has himself contributed to the damage done by the employee. The employing authority was considered to have been negligent in leaving the anaesthetic to an inexperienced doctor without adequate supervision, and damages were awarded in the proportion 80 per cent against the employing authority and 20 per cent against the doctor.

19. (1952) 2 All ER 125; (1952) 2 QB 852.

1953: *Crawford* v. *Board of Governors of Charing Cross Hospital*[20]

Brachial plexus palsy developed during an operation, the patient's arm having been extended and abducted for some two hours while a blood transfusion was being given. The anaesthetist admitted that he had not read an article in *The Lancet* which had referred to this danger, and the plaintiff was awarded £4,000 damages. The Court of Appeal reversed the decision and held that failure to read every article in the medical press did not amount to negligence.

1954: *Hatcher* v. *Black*[21]

The patient sued following a thyroidectomy during which the left recurrent laryngeal nerve was injured. Negligence was alleged in respect of failure to warn the patient of the risk of damage to her voice. Lord Justice Denning instructed the jury:

> 'In the case of an accident on the road there ought not to be any accident if everyone used proper care and the same applies in a factory; but in hospital, when a person goes in who is ill and is going to be treated, no matter what care you use there is always some risk. Every surgical operation involves risks. It would be wrong, and indeed bad law, to say that simply because a misadventure or mishap occurred, thereby the hospital and the doctors are liable. Indeed it would be disastrous to the community if it were so. It would mean that a doctor examining a patient, or a surgeon operating at a table, instead of getting on with his work, would forever be looking over his shoulder to see if someone were coming up with a dagger. For an action for negligence against a doctor is for him like unto a dagger. His professional reputation is as dear to him as his body, perhaps more so, and an action for negligence can wound his reputation as severely as a dagger can his body. You must not therefore find him negligent simply because something happens to go wrong, as for instance if one of the risks inherent in an operation actually takes place or because some complications ensue which lessen or take away the benefits that were hoped for or because, in a matter of opinion he makes an error of judgement. You should only

20. (1953) *The Times*, 23rd April and 8th December.
21. (1954) *The Times*, 2nd July.

find him guilty of negligence when he falls short of the standard of a reasonably skilful medical man. In short, when he is deserving of censure – for negligence in a medical man is deserving of censure.'

And further,

'It is for you to say whether you think that he (the doctor) told her that there was no risk whatever, or he may have prevaricated to put her off as many a good doctor would, rather than worry her. But even if you think that he did tell her, is that a cause for censure?'

The verdict was in the favour of the defendants.

1954: *Roe* v. *Ministry of Health*[22]

This tragic case concerned a leakage of phenol through invisible cracks in ampoules used for spinal anaesthetics which resulted in two patients suffering serious paralysis. Lord Justice Denning said:

'It is so easy to be wise after the event and to condemn as negligence that which was only misadventure. We ought always to be on our guard against it, especially in cases against hospitals and doctors. Medical science has conferred great benefits on mankind but these benefits are attended by unavoidable risks. Every surgical operation is attended by risks. We cannot take the benefits without taking the risks. Every advance in technique is also attended by risks. Doctors, like the rest of us, have to learn by experience; and experience often teaches the hard way. Something goes wrong and shows up a weakness and then it is put right,'

and further:

'We must not condemn as negligence that which is only a misadventure.'

1957: *Phillips* v. *Shea. (Supreme Court of Georgia)*

'It clearly shows that Dr Shea in performing the two operations exercised that degree of care, skill and diligence which any competent surgeon would be required to employ in doing, as here , intricate and dangerous operations . . . This court will not hold that a jury is authorised to find that a competent surgeon is negligent in performing an operation until he (the

22. (1954) 2QB. 1 WLR 128.

> plaintiff) calls some other surgeon to assist him,'

and

> 'More than 2,300 years ago Aristotle in his work *Politics* wrote, "As the physician ought to be judged by the physician so ought men to be judged by their peers", and for centuries the courts of this and other countries have, almost without exception, held that expert medical evidence is required to establish negligence respecting the services a physician or a surgeon renders his patient.'

1957: *Bolam* v. *Friern H.M.C.*[23]

The plaintiff, having consented to ECT, sustained fractures of the pelvis. Negligence was alleged in failure to warn of the possibility of fractures and failure to use relaxants. An expert witness having stated that he was opposed to the routine use of relaxants, Mr Justice McNair said that the plaintiff would have to show that he would have refused treatment if warned, and that the defendants were not negligent if they acted in accordance with a practice which had the support of a responsible body of medical men merely because another body took an opposing view.

1958: *Crivon* v. *Barnet H.M.C.*[24]

A pathologist was held not to be negligent – the case concerned the diagnosis of carcinoma – merely because another pathologist, the head of the department, took a different view.

1959: *Moore* v. *Lewisham Group H.M.C.*[25]

Paralysis of the left leg followed a cholecystectomy performed under spinal anaesthesia. There was a clash of expert opinion on the justification for the use of spinal anaesthesia for such an operation. In finding for the defendants Mr Justice Barry stated:

> 'The courts could do no greater disservice to the community or the advancement of medical science than to place the hallmark of legality upon one form of treatment as opposed to another when there was a difference of informed medical opinion as to their merit.'

23. (1957) 2 All ER 118; 1 WLR 582.
24. (1958) CLY 2283; *The Times,* 19th Nov. CA.
25. (1959) *The Times,* 2nd February.

1959: *Williams* v. *North Liverpool H.M.C. and Ors*[26]

Mrs Williams, an obese patient, was to have thiopentone prior to an operation for varicose veins. Blood having been aspirated, 5 c.c. were injected without visible effect. The doctor realised that a substantial part of the thiopentone injected must have gone into the tissues and injected saline but an abscess developed and negligence was alleged. In the Court of first instance, the Judge found that an excessive quantity had been injected without sufficient certainty that the needle was in the vein and that this amounted to negligence. The Court of Appeal reversed this decision, pointing out that the patient's veins were difficult to find and that fat, being insensitive to pain and the patient not therefore complaining of any pain, the doctor did not have the usual warning that the needle was not in the vein. Further, no answer had been given to the question 'What other steps should the doctor have taken to ensure that the needle was in the lumen of the vein?'

1959: *Junor* v. *McNicol*[27]

A consultant had ordered penicillin but his house surgeon was unaware of the order. The house surgeon then, on his own initiative, prescribed an inadequate amount and was sued in negligence. He was held not to have been negligent on the ground that his duties were to carry out the consultant's instructions, and in the event he had exercised initiative beyond the instructions he had received.

1960: *Chapman* v. *Rix*[28]

A butcher injured himself in the abdomen while boning meat. The defendant thought the wound superficial and sutured it, instructing the patient to report to his own doctor. The peritoneum was in fact penetrated and the patient subsequently died. The High Court found the doctor negligent in failing to communicate directly with the patient's own doctor; the Court of Appeal reversed this decision, and the widow appealed to the House of Lords. It was held that the failure to communicate directly was not negligent but *aliter semble* if the patient had not been instructed to report to his own doctor.

26. (1960) *The Times*, 17th January. 27. (1959) *The Times*, 26th March.
28. (1960) *The Times*, 22nd December, HL.

1960: *Corder* v. *Banks*[29]

A plastic surgeon operated to remove excess fat from below the patient's eyes. The operation was carried out as an out-patient procedure and it was common ground that were bleeding to occur within 48 hours, prompt treatment would be necessary to prevent subsequent disfigurement. In the event, bleeding did occur and the patient's telephone call to the defendant went unheeded. The court held that there was a duty on the surgeon to provide postoperative care and that as this care was to be summoned by telephone, then the surgeon had the duty of seeing that the telephone was efficiently manned so that messages would be relayed to him or his deputy. His failure in this respect was held to amount to negligence and he was therefore held liable in damages for the disfigurement the patient suffered.

1961: *Landau* v. *Werner*[30]

In this case Dr Werner, a psychiatrist, was found to have been negligent in that he had pursued social contacts with his patient which had resulted in emotional damage. Having said that it was up to a doctor to justify treatment that was a complete departure from that which was usual, Lord Justice Upjohn said:

> 'It seems to me that this type of treatment would inevitably produce in the mind of Miss Landau the idea that she might break down the doctor's resistance and that he might at last reciprocate her love. With a patient in Miss Landau's state, that must be the worst possible treatment.'

1963: *Coles* v. *Reading H.M.C.*[31]

A patient with a crushed thumb did not, as instructed by a nurse at a cottage hospital, go to a nearby general hospital for tetanus prophylaxis. A general practitioner who saw the patient later assumed that as the patient had been seen at a hospital the question of tetanus prophylaxis would have been dealt with. The hospital authority was found negligent in that the need to go to the general hospital was not adequately impressed on the patient, and no written instruction was given. The general practitioner was found negligent in failing to make enquiries to check that adequate prophylactic treatment had been given.

29. (1960) *The Times*, 9th April. 30. (1961) *The Times*, 23rd November, CA. 31. (1963) *The Times*, 31st January.

1963: *Stevens* v. *Bermondsey H.M.C.*[32]

A patient was injured owing to the negligence of a road sweeper employed by a local authority. Following treatment by a casualty officer he settled his claim against the authority. Subsequently it was found that his disabilities were greater than had been thought and he took action against the hospital authority in respect of the failure of the casualty officer to diagnose and evaluate his disabilities. It was held that the difference between the settlement figure and the true value of the claim was not recoverable as

> 'a doctor's duty was limited to the sphere of medicine and he had nothing to do with the sphere of legal liability unless he examined with an eye to liability.'

This case appears to conflict with a non-medical case, *Hedley Byrne* v. *Heller,*[33] which may perhaps be followed in preference in any similar future action. This was a case concerned with the advice given by bankers to advertising agents regarding a company's financial status. Acting on the advice, the advertising agents had dealings with the company in question and suffered considerable financial loss. The judgment in this case made it clear that a plaintiff, having acted on advice negligently given, could claim not only for any physical harm caused but for any resulting financial loss. Lord Morris expressed the view that:

> 'If A assumes a responsibility to B to tender him deliberate advice, there could be a liability if the advice is negligently given. I say "could be" because the ordinary courtesies and exchanges of life would become impossible if it were sought to attach legal obligation to every kindly and friendly act. But the principle of the matter would not appear to be in doubt. If A employs B (who might, for example, be a professional man such as an accountant or a solicitor or a doctor) for reward to give advice, and if the advice is negligently given there could be a liability in B to pay damages. The fact that the advice is given in words would not in my view prevent liability from arising. Quite apart, however, from employment or contract, there may be circumstances in which a duty to exercise care will arise if a service is voluntarily undertaken. A medical man may unexpectedly come across an unconscious

32. (1963) *The Times,* 16th May.
33. (1964) *Hedley-Byrne* v. *Heller,* AC 465.

> man who is a complete stranger to him and who is in urgent need of skilled attention: if the medical man, following the fine traditions of his profession, proceeds to treat the unconscious man, he must exercise reasonable skill and care in so doing.'

Lord Devlin in his judgment said:

> 'The interposition of the physical injury is said to make a difference of principle. I can find neither logic nor common sense in this. If, irrespective of contract, a doctor negligently advises a patient that he can safely pursue his occupation and he cannot, and the patient's health suffers and he loses his livelihood, the patient has a remedy. But if the doctor negligently advises him that he cannot safely pursue his occupation when in fact he can and he loses his livelihood, there is said to be no remedy. Unless of course the patient was a private patient and the doctor accepted half a guinea for his trouble: then the patient can recover all. I am bound to say, my lords, that I think this to be nonsense. It is not the sort of nonsense that can arise even in the best system of law out of the need to draw nice distinctions between borderline cases. It arises, if it is the law, simply out of a refusal to make sense. The line is not drawn on any intelligible principle. It just happens to be the line which those who have been driven from the extreme assertion that negligent statements in the absence of contractual or fiduciary duty give no cause of action, have in the course of their retreat so far reached.'

1964: *Schwartz* v. *United States*[34]

This case resulted in the largest malpractice award to date, namely 725,000 dollars. The plaintiff had, in 1944, a radioactive contrast dye injected into a facial sinus. Following discharge from the Services, he sought treatment at a Veterans' Clinic, and though the records were obtained from the original hospital they were apparently not consulted and the opaque substance noted was assumed to be Lipiodol, which is non-radioactive. In 1953, the original hospital record was consulted at an examination for pension purposes but the examining doctor, though aware that the radio-opaque material was radioactive, did not inform the doctor treating the patient.

34. (1964) 230 F. Supp. 536.

Cancer was diagnosed in 1956 and expensive surgery was undertaken. The judge considered the government physicians to have been grossly negligent and awarded exemplary damages, presumably to mark this view. In the event the government settled the case for 200,000 dollars less than the award, the plaintiff preferring to accept this rather than risk an appeal.

1967: *Chin Keow* v. *Government of Malaysia*[35]

A doctor was found to have been negligent in giving an injection of penicillin without having ascertained from the records that the patient was sensitive.

35. (1967) *The Times*, 14th April.

3. Negligence in Diagnosis

The average doctor is unlikely in the extreme to find himself involved in a case such as those referred to in the previous chapter, which marked stages in the development of negligence. Very different, however, is his prospect of receiving a solicitor's letter alleging negligence in respect of some matter in which precedence is all too abundant, for indeed, as in all fields, it is the commonplace that occurs most frequently.

A statistical survey of 500 cases of alleged medical negligence carried out by the author showed the most common causes concerning diagnosis to be cases involving foreign bodies, multiple injuries, and head injuries. The fracture most commonly missed is undoubtedly that of the scaphoid; the dislocation probably that of the hip when it is combined with a fracture of the shaft of the femur or of the tibia and fibula.

How do these cases come about? There are, it is suggested, three all too common findings: failure to take an adequate history, failure to take an X-ray, and in a smaller but significant number of cases, failure to test the urine. Before turning to the cases that make up the bulk of this chapter, a word on each of these failings.

As every clinical teacher has said to every student, the history is all important. An elderly man was brought to a hospital in the north of Ireland late one evening and his companions informed the casualty officer that having had a few glasses of stout, the patient had, on emerging from the bar, felt somewhat off balance and had put his hand out against a passing bus to steady himself. The casualty officer failed to find any injury on examination and discharged the patient, who was found dead the following morning. A moment's thought surely demands that a patient with such a history requires to be kept under observation.

An octogenarian ex-nurse fell down some steps and, when taken to hospital, said that she had felt something go in her hip.

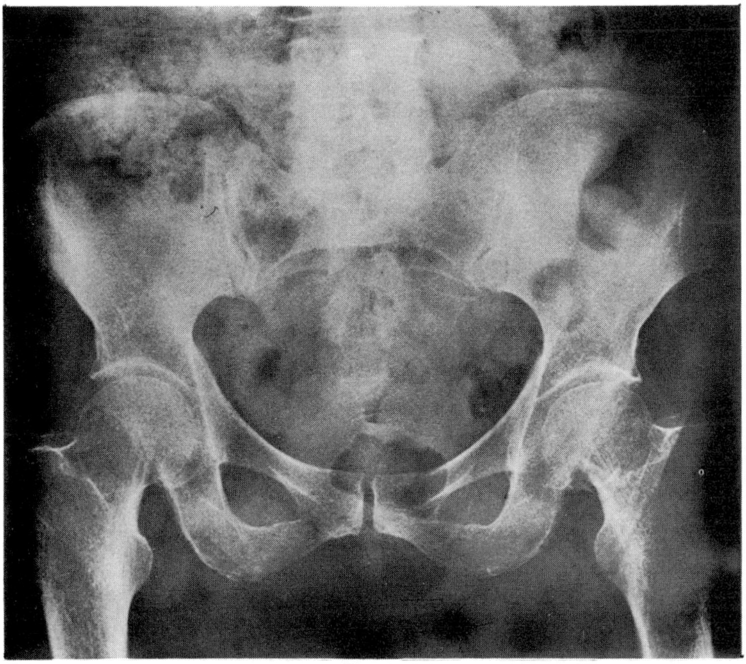
Fig. 1

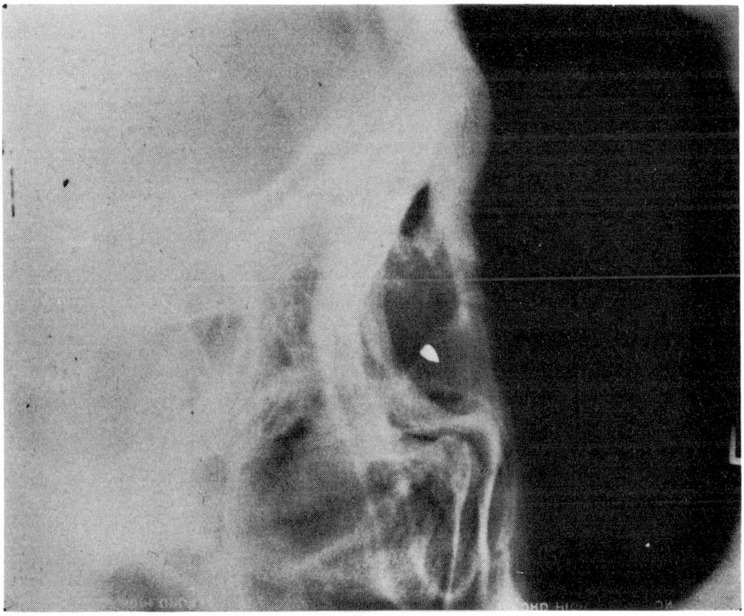
Fig. 2

The casualty officer, failing, very reasonably, to detect the impacted fracture in the X-ray (Fig. 1) discharged her, when she promptly went to another hospital where the diagnosis was made. There is, of course, no rule that says that a patient is not allowed to be right and it is difficult in the extreme to defend an allegation of negligence when the doctor has been presented with the diagnosis in this manner.

Failure to take an X-ray frequently follows from the failure to take an adequate history. All too often the patient's story that he got something in his eye is accepted without further enquiry. Such enquiry will sometimes strongly indicate the possibility of an intra-ocular foreign body. Figure 2 illustrates such a case, where a cartridge gun was being used to fire nails through wood into concrete.

A second cause of failure to X-ray is the very natural tendency to accept the history taken by a previous doctor as being complete. If a wound is not healing, it is important to go back to the beginning and enquire as to the original cause – in this case (Fig. 3), it was not until a third doctor saw the patient that the possibility of a foreign body was considered and the piece of glass discovered on X-ray.

The reasons for not taking an X-ray are known to every doctor – an overworked, understaffed department, no radiographer on the premises at night or weekends, the waiting time for the patient, to name but a few. Obvious as all this may seem, it will avail the doctor naught in court where, should a fracture or foreign body have been missed, he will have difficulty in showing that he used reasonable care and skill.

Failure to test the urine arises more often in general than in hospital practice. Some patients have a remarkable facility for forgetting to bring specimens and being unable to produce them in the surgery. A common sequence of events is that the patient's symptoms indicate the advisability of testing for glycosuria though no probability that sugar will be found. A specimen cannot be produced, the patient omits to bring it, the doctor does not repeat his request, and when the diagnosis is finally made, an allegation of negligence swiftly follows. The one word 'urine' on the patient's notes has more than once evidenced that any fault there may have been did not lie with the doctor.

The rest of this chapter consists of case histories taken

largely from the records of the Medical Protection Society. In presenting these cases it must be realised that settlement is not to be equated with admission of negligence, for many reasons may require that a case should not be contested in court. Adverse publicity, the death of the doctor or of essential witnesses, the

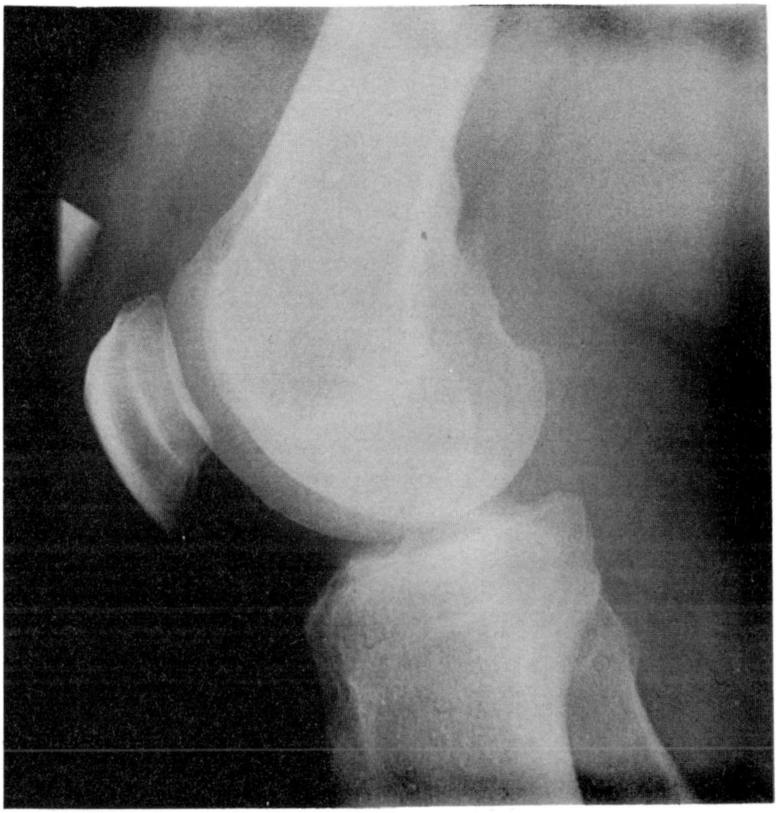

Fig. 3

sympathy of the court towards an injured plaintiff, and the inability to obtain costs against a legally aided plaintiff all combine towards settlement where no point of principle is at stake. At the time of writing the hope has just appeared, in the case of *Hanning* v. *Maitland*[1], that the Judiciary will no longer operate the Legal Aid Act 1964 in such a way as to frustrate the intention of the Legislature, but it is perhaps unlikely that

1. (1969) *The Times*, 12th December.

such bodies as the Medical Protection Society will be allowed to obtain costs against a legally aided plaintiff even though it becomes apparent that the case should never have been brought.

Missed Fractures and Dislocations

A practitioner acting as an assistant had to advise and treat a boy who was on his principal's list. The boy complained of a bruised left heel, saying that he had hurt himself at school by landing heavily on his feet. Since the incident, he had walked with his left heel off the ground and walked in this way when he entered the surgery. After an examination of the foot, during which the doctor could find no physical signs of bony damage or other abnormality, he decided the pain must be due to bursitis. At this stage no mention whatever was made of pain in the left leg or hip. Accordingly, he told the boy to keep the heel off the ground and walk on his toes. Three months later he again saw the boy, who then complained of pain in the region of the left hip, giving a history of having a fall in an ice-rink a week before. There was no limp when he entered the surgery but the doctor decided to have the patient undressed so that the hip joint could be properly examined. He could find no evidence of bruising nor was the joint tender; on the contrary, the pain seemed to be in the gluteal muscles. The leg moved easily without undue or unnatural mobility and there was no apparent shortening. In the abscence of physical signs, and in view of the fact that the hip joint was freely moveable, the doctor saw no necessity for an X-ray examination. After a five months' interval the boy attended again, complaining of soreness and vague aches in the upper and postero-lateral aspects of the left thigh. The doctor made a careful examination of the boy on the couch, putting his hip-joint successfully through a full range of movements. The femur he tested by putting heavy pressure across the shaft, but none of these procedures elicited any pain. At this time the doctor had in mind the possibility of a slipped epiphysis but he came to the conclusion that the condition was purely muscular and made a note to this effect on the record card. Eight months after the original complaint regarding the hip the boy came to the surgery with his mother, and the doctor examined him again but could find nothing amiss. The mother suggested an X-ray examination, but in view of his negative findings the doctor informed her that in his opinion the condition was muscular and that no X-ray examination was indicated.

When he next saw the patient he noticed for the first time that the boy had a definite limp. In view of this he was referred with a letter of introduction to an orthopaedic hospital where it was found that there was a slipped upper left femoral epiphysis.

Subsequently the boy, through his father as next friend, began proceedings against the doctor and his principal in which he alleged that both the doctors were negligent in failing to discover the cause of the condition, namely the slipped epiphysis, and in failing to arrange or give facilities for an X-ray examination at an earlier date. On the advice of experts it was considered wise to explore a settlement, which was effected with the approval of the Court.

The rider of a motor-cycle combination in collision with a motor-car sustained a very severe compound fracture-dislocation of the right ankle and foot, with multiple wounds. On admission to hospital he was found to be wearing an artificial leg, having had an amputation through the upper third of the left thigh some years previously. Although gravely shocked on arrival in the hospital casualty department, the patient was fully conscious and made no reference to pain other than that in his right foot and lower leg. Immediate surgical treatment was necessary and no prior X-ray examinations were made because of the urgency and the obvious nature of the injuries. The fracture-dislocation was reduced and the foot immobilised in wooden splints for the first sixteen days. The stitches were then removed and the foot and ankle immobilised in a plaster extending from below the knee to the toes. During this period there was a reference in the nursing notes to a complaint of a bruise on the side of the thigh on the day after the accident, and the clinical record dated two days after the accident contained the entry 'swelling of thigh less now than last night'. No X-ray examination of the femur or hip-joint had been ordered, although the patient was seen each day by the house officer, and frequently also by the orthopaedic surgeon who performed the operation, and by his registrar.

The patient was discharged home five weeks after the accident with his leg still in plaster, and two months later re-admitted for one week for removal of the plaster, rehabilitation in walking, and a period of intensive physiotherapy. In the following months he was examined by a medical referee acting for an insurance company in conjunction with the surgeon who had treated him. They found he had full movement of the knee joint, but the foot and ankle movements were still seriously restricted and there was gross weakness of the whole leg. Daily physiotherapy was prescribed and he made steady improvement until three months later when it was noticed that he was developing an increasing shortening of the right leg which, on X-ray examination, was found to be due to an un-united fracture of the neck of the femur; there was dislocation of the femur upwards and a new false joint on the ileum. It was decided that operation upon this hip was unlikely to result in improvement, and nine months after the accident it was clear that he would never be able to return to his former employment but must seek work of a sedentary nature to which he could travel by invalid chair.

At this stage, the patient's solicitors issued a writ against the owner and driver of the car that caused the injuries also citing as defendants the hospital and the orthopaedic surgeon, alleging negligence in failing to diagnose and treat the fractured femur until seven months after the accident.

The surgeon's protection society sought the opinion of an independent orthopaedic surgeon, who described the case as 'one of those difficult problems of multiple injuries where the most dangerous lesion to life and limb attracts the concentrated attention of all the surgical team, and undisplaced or impacted fractures and minor injuries are overlooked'. Although he fully appreciated the severity of the ankle and foot injuries, the absence of the opposite leg as a yardstick for comparison, and the initial paucity of symptoms and signs in the region of the right hip, he felt he would be unable to support the omission to have an X-ray examination of this area until more than seven months after the accident. He considered that the treatment of the foot was of the highest efficiency and, no doubt, saved it from amputation but the failure to diagnose and treat the fractured femur earlier had undoubtedly resulted in a serious permanent disability that might have been avoided. He was unable to escape the conclusion that the fracture should have been diagnosed earlier. In the light of these observations there was no alternative but to explore a settlement, the insurers of the motor car owners accepting liability for 45 per cent of the agreed damages.

In December 1957 an army officer, who had been kicked on the forearm by a horse, attended the casualty department of a hospital. An orthopaedic surgeon who chanced to be passing through the department at the time was asked by the casualty officer to see him. Clinically it was clear that there was a fracture of the ulnar shaft caused by the direct blow of the horse's hoof, but the surgeon requested that the X-ray examination should include the elbow joint as well as the bones of the forearm. The films confirmed the presence of a roughly transverse fracture in the middle of the shaft of the ulna with very slight angulation, but the surgeon did not detect any displacement of the head of the radius in either lateral or antero-posterior views. No reduction of the fracture was considered necessary, and a plaster was applied extending from the axilla to the heads of the metacarpals.

Two days later the films were seen by the consultant radiologist who reported the fact that, in addition to the fracture, there was a dislocation of the head of the radius, but unfortunately, the surgeon was not informed of this finding nor was his attention drawn to the report when the patient attended again four weeks later. The X-ray films were not inspected again on this occasion, but the patient was asked to return again in a fortnight for removal of the plaster and further X-ray examination. At the next attendance, the fracture, clinically, seemed to be uniting satisfactorily and there was no local tenderness, but the X-ray film showed little new bone formation. Fourteen days later the plaster was again removed, but as there was neither clinical nor radiological evidence of much change a long arm plaster was reapplied and the patient told to return after a month. At the attendance on 8th March the fracture was clinically united and X-ray films confirmed early bony union. No further splinting was ordered, the arm was left free, and the patient told to avoid strain. When he was seen on 29th March the elbow could not be fully extended nor could it be flexed to an angle of less than 80 degrees; pronation and supination were grossly restricted. Nevertheless, function appeared to be fair in spite of this limitation in the range of movement which was thought to be due, possibly, to some cross union between the radius and ulna as apparently suggested by the X-ray film taken on this occasion.

Continuance of ordinary use by the patient was advised, but when he returned after a fortnight, supination and pronation had not improved so the surgeon ordered further X-ray films to include the elbow joint. He then saw that there was a complete forward dislocation of the head of the radius and, on consulting the patient's records, found that the radiologist's report on the original X-ray film taken in December referred to this condition. The situation was accordingly explained to the patient who was advised that, after allowing some weeks for the consolidation of the ulna fracture, surgical excision of the head of the radius would improve all movements of the elbow joint.

However, the patient decided to consult another surgeon and shortly afterwards instructed solicitors to make a claim against the first surgeon on the grounds that he would have suffered little or no disability if the fracture dislocation had been properly diagnosed in the first instance. As soon as the facts were reported to the protection society the papers were submitted to an expert and, as a result of the latter's opinion, the society agreed that liability could not be denied and instructed their solicitors to negotiate a settlement. When first approached, the patient's solicitors mentioned a sum far in excess of the amount for which the case was finally settled.

A casualty officer saw a patient who complained of pain over the dorsum of his right hand following a fall on a flight of stairs that morning. On examination he could find no swelling and no clinical evidence of bone injury. He strapped the hand and advised the patient to return in two days.

At his next visit, the patient stated there was some improvement and was given a crêpe bandage and told to return if progress was not satisfactory. He continued to work but returned to the hospital about five weeks later as the hand and wrist were painful; seen by the resident surgical officer he was thought to have a fracture of the right scaphoid, and X-ray examination confirmed this injury.

Solicitors consulted by the patient then wrote claiming compensation, alleging that greater care should have been taken in diagnosing the injury; that X-ray examinations should have been made when the patient first attended the hospital, and that his condition had been worsened by his being allowed to continue work and his recovery had thereby been retarded.

The society sought the opinion of an orthopaedic surgeon which was that the delay in immobilising the fracture had not led to any permanent ill-effect as union was satisfactory in eight months but that the rate of union was somewhat slower than it might have been had the injury been diagnosed earlier and the wrist immobilised in plaster from the date of the patient's first visit to hospital.

As a result of this opinion it was agreed that liability could not be denied and a settlement was negotiated.

In a road accident on the 1st March 1958, a lorry driver sustained serious injuries to his right leg. On arrival at the nearest general hospital he was seen by a house surgeon and, later, by the surgical registrar. X-ray examination confirmed a comminuted fracture of the right tibia, a fracture of the shaft of the fifth metatarsal bone, and fractures of the bases of the third and fourth metatarsal bones of the right foot. All wounds were excised and sutured and a plaster splint applied up to the groin. For three weeks progress was uneventful, and although he found movement difficult and complained occasionally of pain in the leg, this was not referred specifically to his hip. On 21st March, when the plaster was changed, the registrar made a note: 'Change of plaster. Wounds healed. Check X-ray; good position.' On 24 March the patient was sent home on crutches and returned, as instructed, a fortnight later to be seen by the consultant under whose care he had been. He was told he could start weightbearing after three weeks, but in fact did not attempt this until 3rd May when he immediately experienced such great pain that an earlier out-patient appointment was arranged. As soon as the consultant saw him on 6th May he diagnosed a dislocated hip (Fig. 4), which was confirmed by X-ray examination. He was promptly admitted to a specialist hospital where four days later an open operation was performed to reduce the dislocation. On 1st July he was discharged and told to report to the general hospital nearer his home. His attendance at this hospital continued at intervals for six months, when he had an operation on the right foot (February 1959). Although his last plaster was removed the following July, he was not able to resume his work as a lorry driver until another twelve months had elapsed. When a writ was served (March 1961) on the Regional Hospital Board,

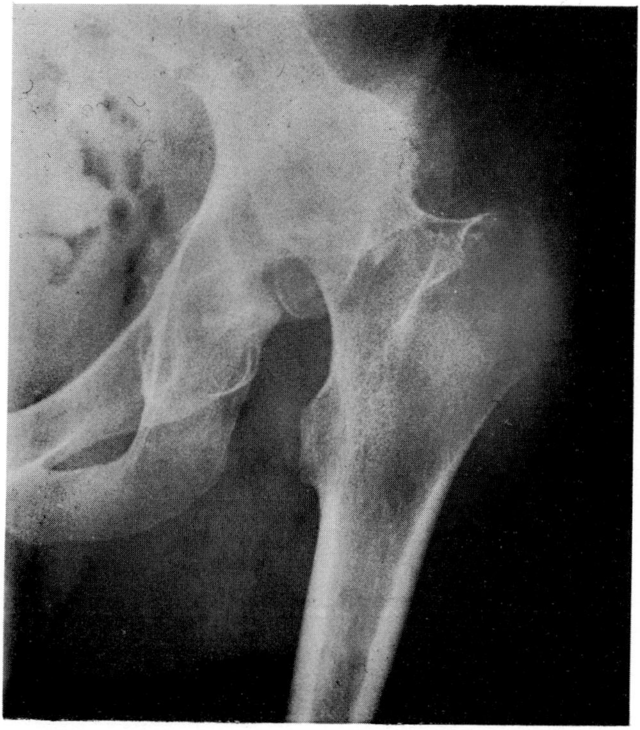

Fig. 4

it was claimed on his behalf that he had suffered a dislocated hip on 1st March 1958, the date of his accident, which should have been noticed when he was examined on admission by the house surgeon and the registrar and, later, by the consultant. A proper examination on any of these occasions, it was alleged, would have disclosed a dislocation which was not in fact diagnosed until 6th May, nine weeks later.

When the case was tried in 1962 the Judge in a meticulous judgment gave a verdict in favour of the defendants. He reviewed at length the evidence of the house surgeon and the consultant and the written statement and notes of the registrar, who had meanwhile emigrated. After referring to the evidence of the surgeon who performed the operation to reduce the dislocation, and carefully assessing the purport of the latter's operation notes made at the time, referred to 'a severe, even startling conflict of medical evidence' between the experts. Those called by the plaintiff testified that there must have been classical signs of dislocation when the patient was admitted to hospital after the accident, and as these had been missed the examining practitioners were negligent.

The Judge however preferred the suggestion of the defendants' expert that with the fracture of the rim of the acetabulum there may have been a partial or temporary dislocation of the hip which 'might well have moved back by itself' only to recur when weightbearing was first attempted nine weeks after the accident.

A provisionally registered house surgeon deputising for the casualty officer was called to see a patient who had suffered an injury to his right hip in a motor-cycle accident. He examined the hip, and an X-ray was taken. No bony injury was seen and, later in the day, the films were examined by a locum consultant radiologist. He reported that there appeared to be a large mass with a calcified periphery at the upper end of the shaft of the femur and a portion of bone detached from some part of the neck. No complete fracture of the neck was seen. The patient was instructed to return home and to rest for a few days, but eighteen days later he was again examined, when it was found that he was unable to walk on his right leg and there was some wasting of the muscles. A further X-ray was then taken, and it disclosed an impacted fracture of the neck of the right femur with rotation of the distal portion. Four days later an operation for insertion of a Smith Petersen pin was successfully performed and the patient was discharged from hospital two weeks later. He had a normal convalescence and was back at work in four months with very few complaints. A year after the operation the pin was removed, and eight months later X-ray examination showed an aseptic necrosis of the head of the femur with considerable deformity. As a result of this a right MacMurray's osteotomy was performed with a very good result. Two and a half years after the initial injury the patient had no local tenderness though still some slight pain.

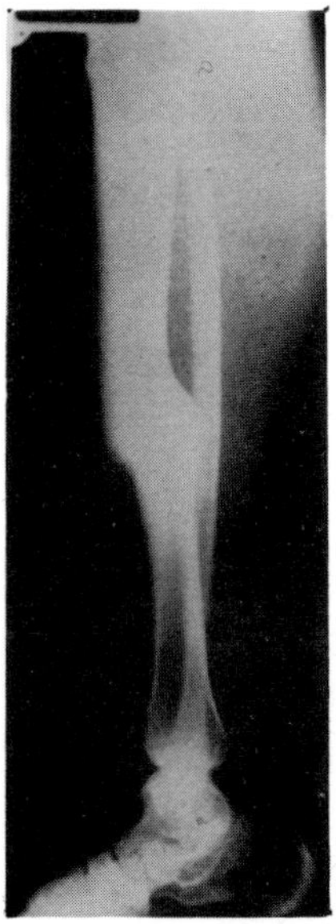

Fig. 5

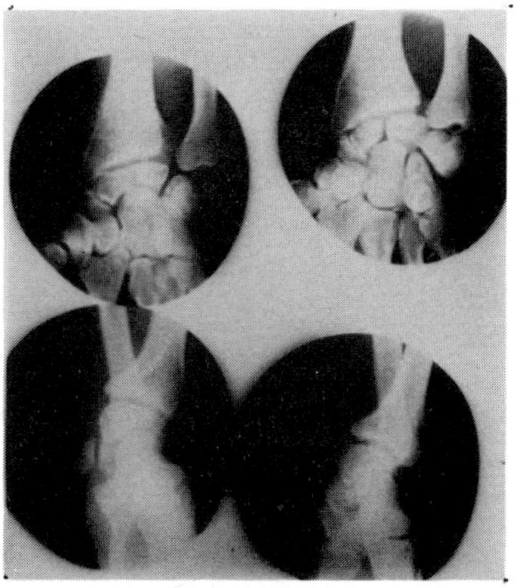

Fig.6

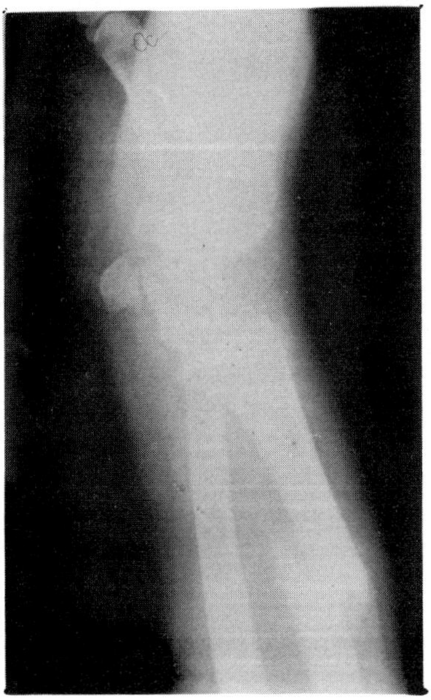

Fig. 7

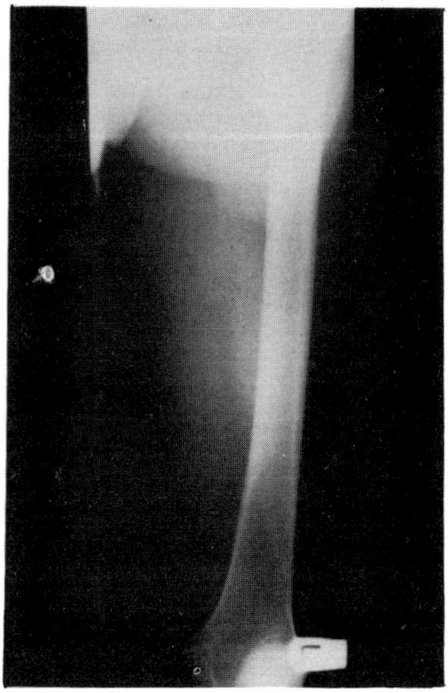

Fig. 8

Three years after the accident the house surgeon received a solicitor's letter claiming negligence on his part, and a writ was issued against him and the hospital management committee. The case was considered by the protection society who had regard to the fact that their member, the house surgeon, had failed to recognise a fracture on a wet film, which the locum consultant radiologist apparently failed to see on a dry film later. The point had been made that one of the films was of poor quality. This suggested that if indeed one of these X-rays was of poor quality then the radiographer and the radiologist who was prepared to report upon it would presumably be the persons at fault. In these circumstances it was decided to deny liability on behalf of the house surgeon. Eventually it was agreed with the patient's solicitors that their client was entitled to damages solely in respect of the delay in treatment and a small payment was shared equally between the hospital authority and the radiologist.

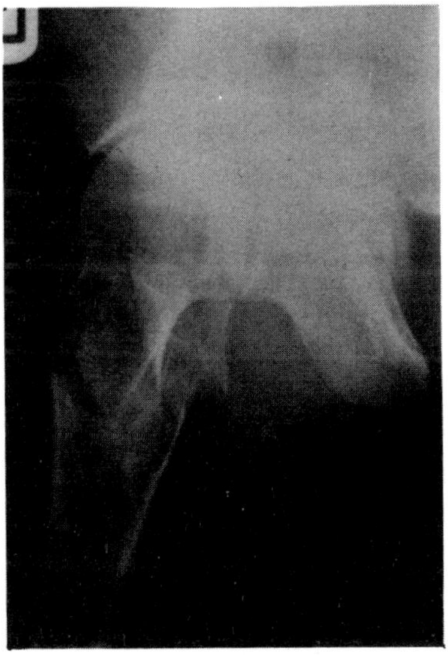

Fig. 9

The history that the patient had been struck by a tramline that he was assisting to remove did not prevent a wound of the leg being treated as a soft tissue one, and it was not until six months after the injury that the X-ray in Figure 5 was taken.

When the X-ray in Figure 6 was taken, the old fracture of the scaphoid was diagnosed, but the dislocation of the inferior radio-ulnar joint and the angulation of the radius were missed. Six weeks later a further X-ray was taken in another hospital (Fig. 7).

No fracture was seen on the X-ray shown in Figure 8.
This one was taken a week later (Fig. 9).

Missed Foreign Bodies

A general practitioner who happened to be attending an emergency in his local hospital was asked to see a casualty suffering from a lacerated wound of the sole of the foot caused by a broken bottle. He cleansed the wound, which was bleeding freely, and arrested the haemorrhage, but was unable to detect any glass fragments. He did not order X-ray examination because he believed his clinical examination had excluded the presence of any foreign body and, moreover, did not think that a glass fragment was likely to be detected in this way. After suturing the wound he instructed the patient to report to his own doctor and heard no more of the matter until a year later he received a letter from the man's Trade Union. This stated that their member who had cut his foot the previous July, was unable to work for eight weeks after the accident and then was fit for light work only. By the following April his foot had become so painful and inflamed that he was admitted to hospital, where a surgeon had subsequently removed a fragment of glass from it.

When the case was undertaken by the protection society it was agreed that if there was any liability it must rest with the practitioner. Meanwhile, the surgeon who actually removed the glass fragment was able to provide further information. Although the original injury had been on the sole of the foot, at the time of his second admission to hospital an abscess was pointing on the dorsum, from which the glass was removed quite easily at operation. The piece of bottle recovered was roughly triangular in shape, its base measuring approximately 1¼ in. in length.

In view of the fact that the foreign body would probably have been revealed by an X-ray examination at the time of the injury, it was decided that it would be unwise to repudiate liability and let this case go to trial. A settlement was therefore agreed with the patient's Trade Union.

A patient was diagnosed as suffering from diverticulitis and a pelvic tumour with symptoms of large bowel obstruction. It was agreed that the surgeon and a gynaecologist should together perform a laparotomy. At operation, fibroids were found, and having completed a hysterectomy the gynaecologist

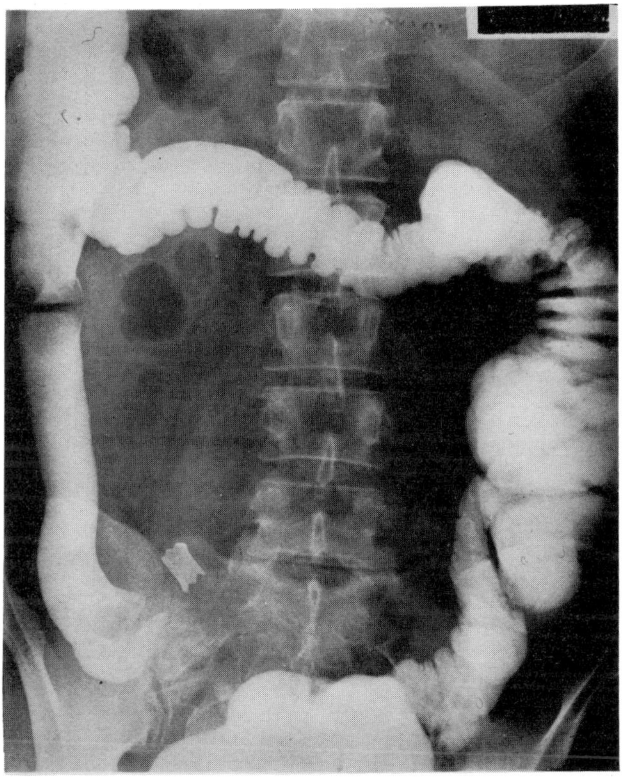

Fig. 10

left the theatre. The surgeon, having found the pelvic colon to be almost completely stenosed, dissected the abnormal segments and performed an end-to-end anastomosis. Convalescence was uneventful and the patient was soon discharged, but some two months later she was readmitted as an emergency with further evidence of bowel obstruction. The surgeon concerned being away on leave at the time, she was seen by a colleague, and improved rapidly on conservative treatment. A straight X-ray of the abdomen was reported as showing a possible foreign body, but its nature was not apparently recognised and the patient was again discharged. On his return from holiday the surgeon saw the patient and the X-ray films and immediately realised that the foreign body was the recognition tag of an abdominal pack (Fig. 10).

The patient was readmitted for the third time and together with the gynaecologist, the surgeon again operated, removing the pack and finding it necessary to resect twelve inches of terminal ileum. On investigation it was found that the senior theatre sister, who had been present at the original operation, had not reported any missing pack and in due course it was agreed that liability should be shared equally between hospital authority and the protection society.

A baby aged 13 months arrived in the casualty department late one afternoon with a note from the general practitioner requesting X-ray films of the chest because of a history of suspected 'swallowed crumb'. The child was apparently in good health, with no respiratory distress, and an X-ray film was taken. This was seen by the casualty officer who could find no evidence of a foreign body on the wet plates; he wrote a note to the practitioner and asked the mother to contact him again. The baby's cough became worse during the evening and the mother telephoned the practitioner's deputy for advice. The next morning, when the consultant radiologist diagnosed a collapse of part of one lung, prompt attempts were made to contact the general practitioner and the parents, so that the child could be seen again immediately, but at about that time the parents had called their doctor urgently. He arrived to find that the child had just died in a paroxysm of coughing. Autopsy revealed that death was due to respiratory obstruction caused by an orange pip lodged at the carina (Fig. 11).

The child's parents claimed damages alleging negligence on the part of the casualty officer, and while expertise in the interpretation of X-rays (especially wet films) cannot reasonably be expected of a recently qualified doctor, the appearance of the film in this case was such that it was felt that he should have obtained a more experienced opinion at the time. The claim was settled.

A boy of thirteen was knocked off his bicycle by a car. On examination he showed quite extensive bruising, with grazing of the head, face, elbows and hands, and a lacerated wound extending into the muscles of the right buttock. The wounds

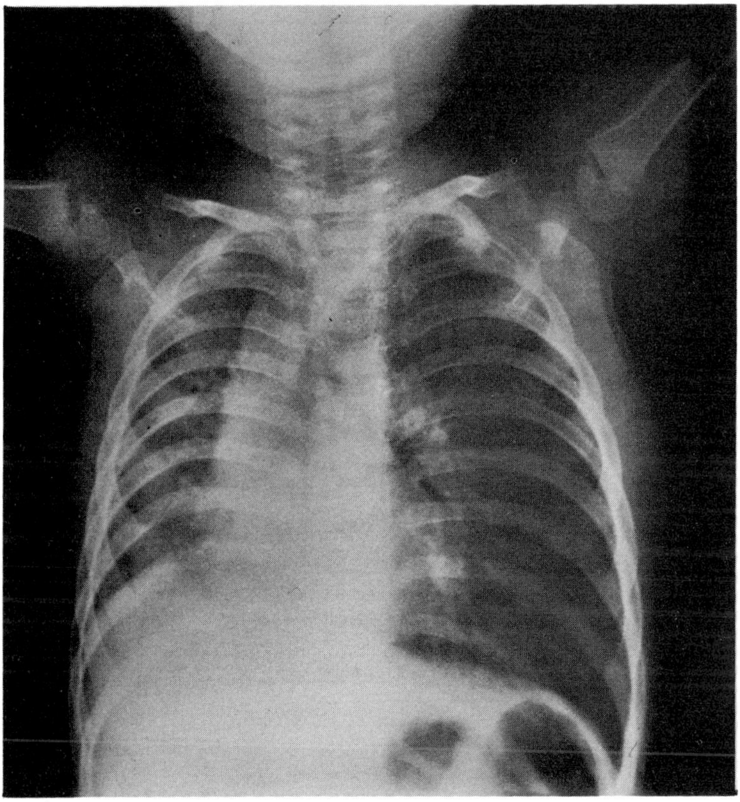

Fig. 11

were dressed, and toilet and suture of the buttock laceration performed under a local anaesthesia. All seemed well following this treatment until three months later when the patient presented with a cystic swelling in the sacral region. The boy was unusually plump for his age and it seemed that he had a haematoma, which was aspirated in the outpatient department, and he was asked to attend again in one week. This he did not do, but two months later he was seen again with a recurrence of the haematoma. On this occasion a radiograph was taken for the first time and revealed to everyone's surprise a large foreign body, which appeared to be a car door handle, lying deeply in the tissues (Fig. 12). This was subsequently removed and the wound healed normally without any after effects.

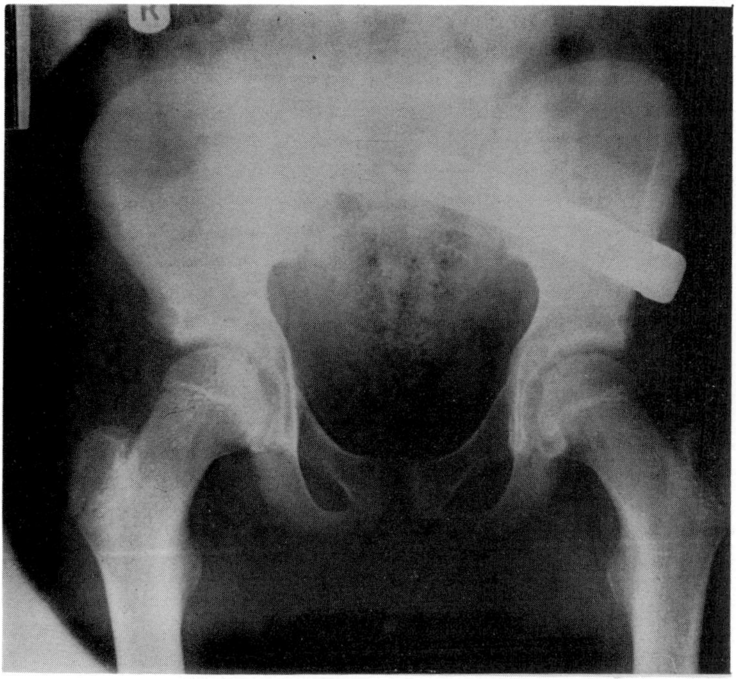

Fig. 12

Although the doctor had no reason to suspect that any large foreign body had entered the wound, and certainly nothing so large as a door handle, and although he seemed to have explored the wound at the time of the suture, yet it could not be denied that such an object should not have remained undiscovered and that a settlement should therefore be effected. As the boy had not suffered any significant disability between the time of the accident and the subsequent removal of the foreign body, settlement was effected for a comparatively small amount.

A forty-one-year-old welder with a lacerated lip was treated by a casualty officer. The doctor obtained a history that the laceration was caused by a steel nail. Examination revealed a half-inch laceration at the muco-cutaneous junction of the upper lip, which the casualty officer sutured. The patient

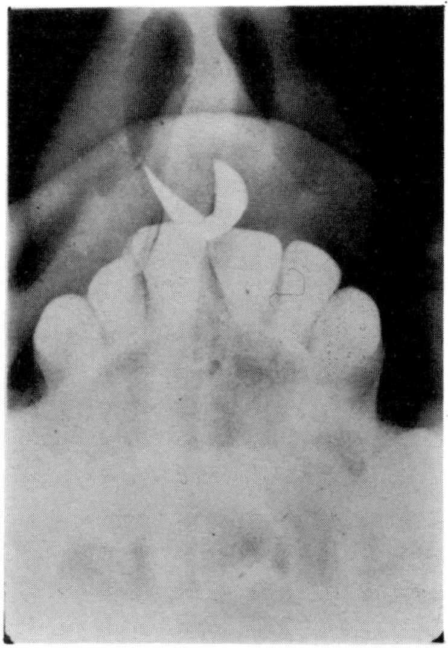

Fig.13

returned a week later. The laceration had healed, the sutures were removed and he was discharged.

Three weeks later, however, the patient returned to the casualty department because the healed scar was still very tender. A retained foreign body was suspected, and this was confirmed by X-ray. It was discovered that at the time of the injury the welder had been working with a steel punch that burst, causing a fragment to lodge in his lip (Fig. 13). This was easily removed under local anaesthesia. Although the patient had not been aware of any fragment entering his lip an adequate history must have suggested the possibility, and the subsequent claim for damages was settled.

A patient suffered a laceration of his thigh while working with a wood-cutting machine. An X-ray (Fig. 14) was taken and the

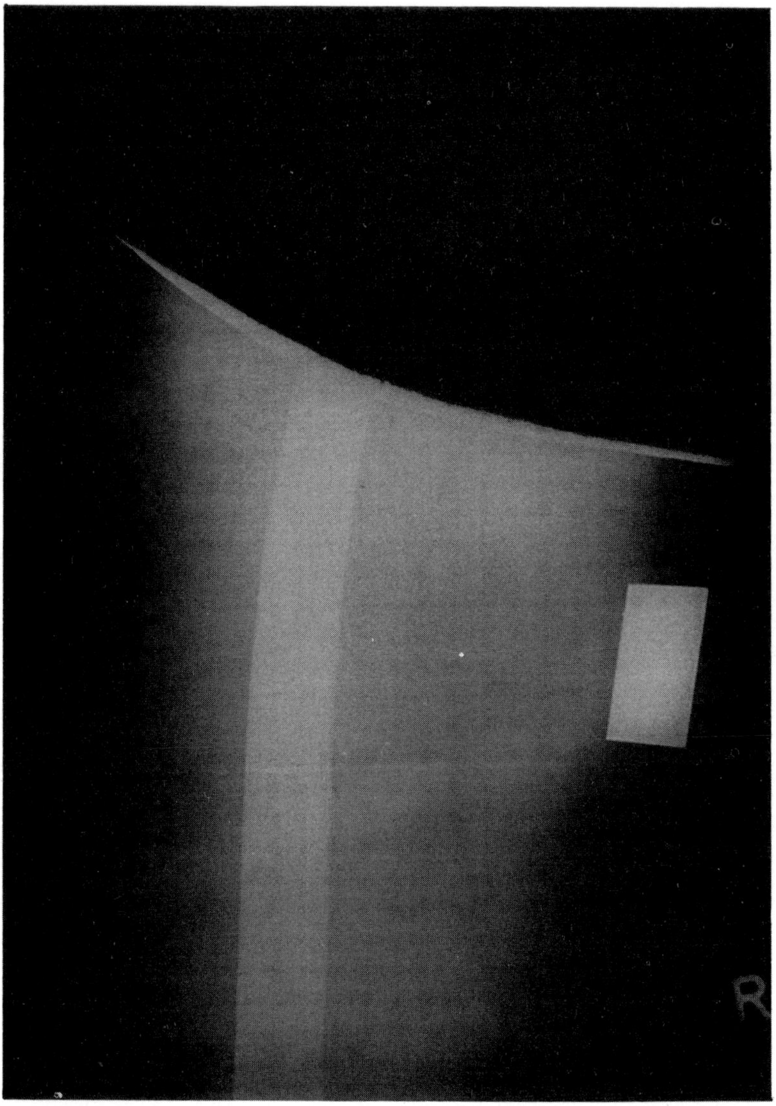

Fig. 14

wound sutured. Some eighteen months later a foreign body became apparent clinically, and what had been thought to be an artefact was indeed the blade of the cutter.

Miscellaneous

A shipyard worker in Scotland, who sustained a fall at his work, was taken to hospital and carefully examined by the casualty officer who found a laceration of the forehead, a fractured left wrist, and possible fractures of the left lower ribs. He was referred for X-ray examination and the radiologist reported that the films confirmed the fractured wrist and disclosed a fracture of the seventh rib, but that no fracture of the skull was seen. The casualty officer put the wrist in plaster, strapped the chest, sutured the laceration and, as there was no clinical evidence of either intra-cranial or intra-thoracic injury, sent the patient home by ambulance with instructions to report to the fracture clinic the following morning. When he did so he was seen by an orthopaedic surgeon who confirmed the findings on the casualty record card, re-dressed the laceration, enlarged the wrist plaster, and again sent the patient home by ambulance with instructions to report back a week later. That evening the family doctor was called in and administered morphine to deaden pain, but the patient's condition deteriorated and he died at about 6.15 the following morning.

At autopsy there were revealed a fracture of the base of the skull with subarachnoid bleeding, fractures of the fifth, sixth, seventh, and eighth ribs on the left side, with complete collapse of the left lung, the lower lobe having a superficial laceration. The pathologist expressed the opinion that death was due to fracture of the skull and ribs, a left-sided pneumothorax and subarachnoid haemorrhage, and this was adopted by the jury, who returned a formal verdict at the Fatal Accident Enquiry ordered by the Procurator-Fiscal.

In due course the widow and two daughters of the deceased brought an action for damages against the hospital, alleging negligence by the hospital doctors in failing to diagnose the fractured skull and the intra-thoracic damage, and in failing to admit the patient for observation.

After careful consideration of the evidence contained in the hospital records and given at the Fatal Accident enquiry, the protection society decided that the action should be defended, and this decision was justified by the judgment of the Court of Sessions in favour of the defenders after a trial lasting four days. In this judgment the Judge found specifically that neither the subarachnoid bleeding nor the pneumothorax had made its appearance while the patient was at the hospital and that, 'the evidence does not establish any practice of automatically detaining a man who has suffered a head injury (without losing consciousness) or a rib injury. Apart from practice, reliance can only be placed on signs apparent at the time of the examination. It is not enough in order to establish negligence to show that other medical men would on those signs have acted differently'.

An elderly man was brought to a hospital casualty department after he had collapsed at the roadside when returning from work. A bus was passing at the time but nobody appeared to have seen it strike him. He was examined by the casualty officer, who found him very shocked but fully orientated and able to answer questions. He said he felt all right, but added that he had been feeling 'queer' all that afternoon. Examination disclosed no abnormality in his central nervous system or cranial nerves and his chest and pelvis could both be compressed without causing him pain. No marks or abnormalities were found on his skull, and the only external mark of violence anywhere was a small abrasion on the outer side of his left knee. He was thercfore allowed to go home and instructed either to call in his own doctor or return to the hospital if he felt unwell.

At 10 a.m. the next day the patient was readmitted at the request of his general practitioner, who stated that the man had been unconscious all night. When examined on the second occasion he was deeply unconscious and it was seen that a large haematoma had developed over the right ear. There was also bruising over the left wrist and the upper part of the right arm, and of the right loin. His comatose state, non-reacting pupils and extensor plantar responses, suggested increased intracranial pressure. X-ray films taken at the bedside did not show any fracture of the skull. The condition of the patient continued to deteriorate and he died at about 8 p.m. the same evening.

At the inquest, the pathologist gave evidence that there was a linear fracture of the vault of the skull, a large extradural haematoma haemorrhage in the frontal lobes of the brain, and fractures of three ribs. The cause of death was stated to be hypostatic bronchopneumonia, due to coma arising from the extradural haematoma.

Less than two months later the casualty officer received a solicitor's letter alleging negligence in his treatment of the deceased and claiming damages on behalf of the widow. The protection society's solicitors were instructed to deny liability and after some months were served with a writ which, in addition to the casualty officer, cited the hospital management committee, and the owners of the bus. The last named settled the claim against them before the action came to trial, but the society and the hospital management committee decided to continue to defend the action.

At the trial there was a conflict of evidence and one of the police witnesses stated that he had twice told the doctor that the deceased had been knocked down by a bus, which the latter denied.

In his judgment the Judge said that the only allegation of negligence against the doctor was that he did not properly examine the deceased and did not ascertain accurately the history before he allowed him to go home. He stated that he had come to the conclusion that the doctor did not understand at the time of his examination that the deceased had been knocked down by a bus and that he found it extraordinarily hard to believe that if this fact had been communicated to him he would not have made a note of it and admitted the man. In the circumstances, therefore, he was justified in sending the patient home with instructions to refer to his own doctor. Judgment was given for the defendants with costs.

Dr A, a general practitioner, examined a young man with a persistent cough and referred him to hospital for investigation of his chest. A few days later the patient met Dr B, his partner, the doctor he usually consulted, on his rounds, and asked if any report had been received. Dr B did not know but instructed him to enquire at the surgery about its receipt and wait for a consultation as soon as it was available. The patient made two enquiries of the receptionist but was told each time that the report had not been received.

He did not attend again until a year later when he saw Dr B and once more complained of cough. No trace could be found of any report from the hospital about the previous X-ray examination, though there was a negative report on his sputum. He was again referred to hospital when it was reported that gross deterioration had occurred and there was widespread disease, with cavitation in the upper two-thirds of the right lung, and infiltration in the left middle and lower zones, whereas 13 months earlier the tuberculous infiltration had been confined to the right upper zone. Following admission to a sanatorium he was treated surgically and remained as an in-patient for some two-years.

In due course he complained to the Executive Council that his doctor had failed to follow up the first report and that if this had been done the progress of the disease might have been arrested. The Medical Services Committee found that Dr B was at fault and recommended that he be censured. Dr B then received a letter from solicitors instructed by the patient claiming damages, and the society decided to repudiate liability and defend the action.

At the trial two years later, evidence was given by the plaintiff confirming the facts quoted above and saying that on the second occasion when he saw the receptionist he was told that since no report had been received he could take it that everything was in order. This evidence the court accepted. It also emerged that the hospital had sent a report of the first X-ray examination to Dr A.

In a long and detailed judgment the judge said that the defendant was the victim of circumstances and his own good nature. Although this might explain the failure to provide treatment urgently required it was not sufficient to answer the charge of negligence by the plaintiff. It was not the plaintiff's fault that his own doctor only learned of his (the patient's) illness while on his rounds – his partner should have passed on the information; and as the defendant admitted he was impressed by the seriousness of what he had learned at this chance meeting he should have expected a report from the hospital, and when this failed to arrive he should have made some enquiry about it. Reasonable care demanded this and he therefore found him liable in damages. The judgment concluded:

> 'While that is my conclusion in law on the facts proved before me, I fully appreciate how unfortunate the combina-

> tion of circumstances was for the defender. I wish to emphasize that no moral blame attaches to him. The facts of this case do not cast any unfavourable reflection upon his professional competence and skill, and do not suggest that he did not endeavour to meet the demands of a large and heavy practice. He was a witness of outstanding candour and sincerity.'

A general practitioner's assistant saw a girl, aged 11, with pain in her right ankle, which he diagnosed as a sprain and treated by applying an elastoplast bandage. There was no improvement two days later and he decided that the condition was due to inflammation and not of traumatic origin. Two days after this he diagnosed cellulitis for which he prescribed a course of penicillin and sulphonamides. Ten days later an abscess which had formed was incised and a large quantity of pus evacuated. Penicillin and local fomentations were continued but a swelling which developed higher up the leg was, in turn, incised.

During the next three months there was a slow improvement, and at one point the girl's father expressed anxiety at the slow progress and asked if an X-ray examination was advisable but the doctor reassured the parents, expressing the view that the inflammatory process involved soft tissues only, and radiography would serve no useful purpose. The illness which had started in the spring was still unresolved in the autumn and the father again complained to the doctor about his conduct of the case and requested an X-ray examination and specialist opinion. The child was then referred to hospital, where radiographs revealed the presence of chronic osteomyelitis with extensive destruction of bone for which appropriate surgical treatment was initiated, and after nine months the orthopaedic surgeon reported that he had overcome the loss of thc tibia and non-union by means of substitution grafts and a cross-bow graft.

When the doctor received this report the parents had transferred to the list of another practitioner but no complaint was made until two years later when the father wrote to the Executive Council who decided that the complaint was so far out of time that it was wholly unreasonable to hold an official enquiry.

After the lapse of another two years the doctor received a solicitors' letter alleging that he had been negligent in refusing the child's father's request for X-ray examination and a second opinion and had thereby prolonged the child's illness. At this stage the protection society was consulted and in due course a County Court summons was issued claiming a modest sum which was met.

The respective responsibilities of surgeon and anaesthetist became a vital issue for consideration in a case that occurred in the southern hemisphere. An elderly sanatorium patient with a twenty-two-year history of pulmonary tuberculosis was referred by the superintendent to a surgeon in respect of a Dupuytren's contracture. The patient was advised to have an operation because he was a painter, but he did not wish to have this done at the time and saw the surgeon again five months later, when his name was placed on the waiting list. After a further five months he was admitted and the notes written by the surgeon stated 'Dupuytren's contracture left; old T.B.', the latter underlined. Pre-operative examination by the house surgeon showed moderate respiratory excursion, harsh breath sounds, crepitations at both apices, no dullness, and moderate emphysema. Although the anaesthetic registrar examined the patient on the day of the operation and ordered a chest X-ray this, for some undisclosed reason was not available before he started the anaesthetic; moreover his examination was not recorded in the notes. For induction he used 0.4 grammes of thiopentone followed by 500 c.c. of Cyclopropane with 5 litres of oxygen, but laryngeal spasms developed necessitating further oxygen and some fluothane. An hour and a half later, as the operation was concluding, the patient suffered a sudden respiratory collapse and, in spite of the usual resuscitative measures, died a few hours later. The pathologist gave the cause of death as respiratory insufficiency and described gross tuberculous lesions in both lungs together with some right ventricular hypertrophy. At the inquest the anaesthetic registrar stated that he had not been aware of the history of tuberculosis, and that had he been he would have sought further advice before administering the anaesthetic. Not long after the Coroner's verdict that death had resulted from respiratory insufficiency resulting from an operation, a claim was lodged on behalf of the widow. It was felt that whereas the superintendent of the sanatorium might well have commented on the patient's fitness for inhalation anaesthesia, nevertheless in view of the time lapse he could in no way be held liable. As the surgeon had noted the pulmonary tuberculosis in his out-patient notes and directed attention to it by underlining he was regarded as entitled to rely upon the anaesthetist satisfying himself as to the man's fitness for anaesthesia. The house surgeon it was considered should have drawn the attention of the anaesthetic registrar to his findings and the previous notes and have arranged for a chest film to be available. To that extent there would seem to have been a breakdown in the chain of administration in the hospital for which the hospital authority should assume responsibility. The major responsibility, however, was considered to rest on the anaesthetic registrar. The notes were there to be consulted, and to be unaware of the previous tuberculous infection, he must have failed to take any worth while history from the patient. A settlement was therefore deemed proper and the hospital's insurers made a contribution.

A pre-registration house physician was standing in for casualty duty one afternoon when he was called to see a man of late middle-age brought in by ambulance, with a complaint that he had collapsed. The doctor found that only two hours earlier the patient had been in the casualty department when the casualty officer had examined and discharged him, finding nothing abnormal. There was also a history that a month previously this patient had, twice in the same day, presented himself at the casualty department when he had been found the worse for drink, on the second occasion being taken away by the police. The house physician carried out a rapid examination, noted a slight bruise on the right side of the scalp, kept the patient in the department for an hour, and then permitted him to go home by ambulance. The ambulance men later returned to say that they had had some difficulty in getting the patient out of the ambulance and into his home, and that his speech at that time had not been normal. The doctor took no action on this information, and a short while later a general practitioner telephoned him to ask about the patient's condition saying that the man's wife had inquired. He assured the practitioner that he had found nothing abnormal and that there had been no reason to admit the patient. About five hours after the patient had been permitted to go home, he was brought back to the Casualty Department by a doctor working for a deputising organisation who had been called to see him, found him deeply unconscious, and had made the provisional diagnosis of pontine haemorrhage. The patient was thereupon admitted, and the condition was diagnosed by the house physician as a case of cerebral haemorrhage; he died some seven hours later not having regained consciousness. Post-mortem examination showed an extra-dural haemorrhage. In due course a claim was made alleging negligence against the casualty officer and the pre-registration house physician. It was apparent that the case was mainly against the latter and while it was appreciated that a person of his experience had been faced with a problem that might well have taxed one many years his senior, nevertheless it was felt that negligence could not be denied.

Whereas it might have been reasonable for the casualty officer to discharge the patient in the first place, the very fact that he was brought back by ambulance with a vague history of collapse, and had a bruise of the scalp, should, it was felt, have led the house physician either to detain the patient, taking an X-ray of the skull, or seek the advice of some senior person.

Again, when the ambulance orderly returned to say that the patient's condition had deteriorated between his leaving the department and arriving home, it could not be considered satisfactory that the doctor took no steps either to have the patient brought back or to ask his general practitioner to visit him. The third failure arose when the general practitioner telephoned; here was evidence that the patient's condition had deteriorated for the third time during the day, and steps should have been taken to see that he was further examined. By the time the patient was brought back to the department and admitted, in all probability it was too late to take any remedial action, so the failure to consider the diagnosis of extra-dural haemorrhage at that time was probably irrelevant. In all the circumstances it was decided that the doctor's interest would be best served by seeking a settlement, and this was arrived at for a moderate sum.

A patient complaining of pain in her left lower jaw was referred to an ENT consultant who requested X-rays of the temporo-mandibular joints and sinuses. The radiologist reported a slight diminution of movement of the joints and that the sinuses were clear, adding that an unerupted lower molar was present on the left side. Having been referred to a dental surgeon, the patient had new full dentures constructed in the hope of relieving the pain, but when seen again some weeks later her symptoms were persisting and it was decided to remove the buried tooth. The patient was admitted and the operation conducted under general anaesthesia, but extensive drilling failed to locate the tooth. Subsequently a further X-ray showed the tooth to be in the right lower jaw and it was found that, of the six films previously taken, the only one that clearly showed the tooth was incorrectly labelled.

The patient unfortunately developed an area of anaesthesia of the lower lip resulting from this operation and it was not long before a claim alleging negligence was lodged by her solicitors. Investigation of the case showed that the film in question had been incorrectly labelled by a radiographer, which fact had not been observed by the radiologist.

Independent opinion was sought in respect of the actions both of the dental surgeon and of the radiologist. As to the former, the expert consulted felt that the surgeon before operating, did not have sufficient radiographic evidence of the exact location of the tooth, and that he should, therefore, have requested a lateral view which would have revealed the error in the marking. This report appeared to some extent to be favourable to the radiologist who pointed out that he was reporting to an ENT surgeon, and that he had not, in fact, been asked to report on the dental condition at all. It was therefore not within his realisation that his report could form the whole basis for a dental operation, and had he not mentioned the tooth he could hardly have been criticised. The radiologist from whom an expert report was sought, however, felt that it would be impossible in court to contend that the non-agreement of the markers on the films should not have attracted the notice of the radiologist.

Meanwhile, a Writ and Statement of Claim were issued against the dental surgeon, the radiologist, and the hospital authority, and very protracted negotiations ensued, due largely to later unfortunate developments in the patient's condition. Some fifteen months after the first operation it became necessary to remove the tooth from the right lower jaw, and seven months later a peripheral neurectomy was carried out on the left side to relieve the hyperaesthesia, sensitivity to cold, and burning sensation the patient was experiencing. This led to marked improvement, but later, due no doubt to regeneration, the symptoms returned, and finally, some three and a half years after the original operation, a resection of the peripheral portion of the left inferior dental nerve was carried out. Although this left the patient with a larger area of complete anaesthesia, combined with a tendency to dribble from the corner of the mouth, and difficulties with food debris lodging in the sulcus, the patient felt that this was a substantial improvement on her previous disability.

The clinical condition having stabilised, it became possible to negotiate a settlement for a sum which, though substantial, was not unreasonable in all the circumstances; the protection society contributed two-thirds having regard to the radiologist and the dental surgeon, the remainder being borne by the hospital authority in respect of the radiographer.

A patient of thirty-seven, after some heavy drinking apparently fell downstairs in his own house in the early hours of the morning. During the day he experienced some difficulty in micturition, and the urine was noted as being 'brown'. He was seen by his doctor who, at first, decided to treat him at home, but after the appearance of the urinary symptoms had him admitted to hospital.

On examination in the casualty department, before admission to the ward, he was found to have several minor bruises and grazes, consistent with his history of a fall, and quite severe bruising of the penile urethra. Subsequent examination of the urine showed blood to be present. In view of the diagnosis of extensive urethral bruising, with the rather remote possibility of a ruptured urethra, he was taken to the ward for observation.

Three days later he was seen by the surgical registrar, but by then the symptoms appeared to have subsided and the patient fit for discharge. In the notes the registrar wrote: 'Urine clear. Passing urine satisfactorily. No further bleeding. No other symptoms. Discharge.' However after a further three days he was admitted once again, having been discovered in the early hours of the morning lying on the floor calling for help. It appeared that he had had another fall, and so severe was the degree of collapse that a provisional diagnosis of paraplegia was made. All treatment proved unavailing, and the patient died soon after admission. Post-mortem examination revealed a tear in the bladder vault about 5 cm long with half to one litre of straw-coloured fluid in the peritoneal cavity.

It was maintained by the relatives that the rupture of the bladder had occurred at the time of the first fall – six days before death – and that it should have been diagnosed and treated on first admission. This was strenuously denied, as it was considered that the history was entirely in keeping with a second injury causing rupture of a probably over-filled bladder, with resultant massive collapse, and that it was not possible that the patient could have carried on if the bladder had been ruptured at the time of the initial injury. At the trial, evidence was elicited from the wife to the effect that he had very great difficulty in walking when he was discharged from the ward, difficulty in carrying his hold-all, so that she had to carry it for him, and he had asked his wife to slow down while walking down a long corridor. When they reached the porter's lodge they had felt it necessary to call a taxi-cab. This evidence seems to have impressed the court much more than that of any expert explaining the very great difficulties involved in proving that the bladder had been ruptured at the time of the first admission. The court took the view that the wife's evidence was substantially correct, that the registrar had therefore discharged the patient when he was 'exceptionally ill', that the bladder was already ruptured on his first admission to hospital, and that the failure to diagnose this was due to lack of care. The finding was in favour of the relatives and substantial damages were awarded.

As in so many cases the defence was hampered throughout by the relative paucity of medical notes. The trial took place three years after the event and with the best will in the world it was obviously very difficult to be certain and accurate without documentary confirmation. Had full clinical notes been available, the conduct of the case would have been greatly assisted and the outcome might well have been in the registrar's favour.

A general practitioner standing in for his partner, the local police surgeon, was called to the police station one afternoon to examine a driver whose car, it was later reported, had mounted the pavement, knocked down a 'No Waiting' sign, and finished up against a wall. The driver admitted to having had one pint of beer and three whiskies some two or three hours previously. The pulse rate was found to be somewhat increased and his breath smelt of alcohol, but co-ordination was reasonably good. The doctor took a blood specimen, considered the driver was sobering up, and concluded that he was not, at the time of the examination, under the influence of alcohol to the extent that his ability to drive was impaired. No injury or illness was found. Somewhat to the doctor's surprise the blood alcohol level was found to be 274 mg/100 ml, and he then changed his opinion regarding the motorist's fitness to drive. The police preferred a charge under Section 6 of the Road Traffic Act and when the case was called in the Magistrate's Court the accused elected to go for trial at Quarter Sessions.

Here the accused pleaded guilty to a charge of dangerous driving, and a small fine was imposed but, so far as driving under the influence was concerned, his Counsel did not find the blood alcohol content any great embarrassment. The court was informed that on the evening prior to the accident the accused had been at a party, during the course of which he had been picked up and squeezed by a large rugby forward and that this had resulted in a rib being fractured. At the time of the accident the accused was experiencing a feeling of constriction in the chest due, presumably, to the fracture being aggravated by his being a heavy smoker, and this, when an on-coming car pulled out to overtake and forced him to swerve, had led to his losing control of the car. This story was supported by an X-ray film taken a day or two after the accident which, on very close inspection, showed an incomplete fracture of the anterior end of the left 7th rib. The evidence for the prosecution was described as being so slender and unsatisfactory that it should not be put to the jury, and despite the high blood alcohol reading the prosecution accepted the plea of not guilty.

Some months later, however, the doctor was surprised to receive a lengthy letter from the accused man's solicitors. This was to the effect that Counsel who had defended the action had advised that the accused had a right of action against the doctor for the recovery of damages amounting to the larger part of the costs of the defence plus an amount in respect of the stress involved by the trial. Negligence was alleged against the doctor in no fewer than eight particulars, including failure to diagnose the fractured rib, failure to diagnose bruising of the knees, failure to arrange for a second urine test, and also in wrongly swabbing the arm with spirit prior to taking the blood sample. The letter went on to say that a test at a London hospital had shown that swabbing with spirit could result in a reading of 300 mg/100 ml when no alcohol at all had been taken. In conclusion it was suggested that the doctor should, to avoid further litigation, pay £600 towards the cost of the defence.

In forwarding the solicitors' letter to his protection society the practitioner admitted that he had used a spirit solution to swab the arm but stated that he had allowed the spirit to evaporate before inserting the needle. None of the other instances of alleged negligence appeared to have any substance.

The society were therefore faced with the novel proposition that a motorist charged with driving under the influence of drink and subsequently acquitted could have a claim against the doctor who examined him on behalf of the police. For such a claim to succeed it would be necessary, first, to prove negligence, and secondly, to prove that it was that negligence that had led to the plaintiff being prosecuted. Considering that trial at Quarter Sessions in such a case is dependent on many factors such as the opinion of the police, the decision of the accused on the advice of his solicitors that he should go for trial, and the possible mishandling of the case by the solicitors before the Magistrates, such a plaintiff would have an uphill task in proving that his loss and damage followed from the doctor's negligence.

To test, therefore, whether this claim was merely a 'try-on', and at the same time to clarify the one point on which the member was possibly open to criticism, the solicitors were invited to put the protection society in touch with the London hospital where the blood alcohol test was said to have taken place. Receipt of this letter was acknowledged but after this there followed complete silence.

A senior registrar in cardiology was, together with a consultant radiologist, undertaking a pre-operative cardiac catheterisation. The patient, who suffered from both mitral and aortic valvular disease, had three catheters inserted which were kept free of clots by saline drips. There were two drips feeding the three catheters, one of the drips being on automatic supply, the other regulated by a hand pump. Pressures having been taken, the radiologist was preparing to take cine X-ray films when the senior registrar, watching a monitor screen, saw a large translucency within the heart shadow. Immediate investigation showed that the saline bottle on automatic feed was empty and oxygen under pressure had entered the heart. Attempts made to withdraw the oxygen were unsuccessful, and the patient succumbed.

An inquest was held, and the Coroner stated that the tests had been necessary and properly performed and the post-mortem had shown that the deceased was a poor operation risk with a short life expectancy.

Allegations of negligence were made against the hospital authority, and as it was clear that liability could not be denied, the question of proportionate liability between the hospital authority on behalf of the technician, the consultant radiologist and the senior registrar had to be determined. The technician had the primary care of the bottles, but was watching recordings at the relevant time, and the darkened room made matters difficult for him. He was, moreover, working under the doctors, though, being experienced, functioned very largely on his own; moreover it was not clear which of the doctors present would in fact give him any necessary instructions.

Settlement was agreed upon and the protection society's offer of 25 per cent on behalf of the registrar was accepted by the hospital authority.

A casualty officer saw a child who had injured her finger a few days previously. He requested X-ray examination and the films were seen by a colleague, who diagnosed a fracture of the middle phalanx and instructed a staff nurse to strap the finger to an adjoining one. The strapping, it was stated should remain in place for about nine days and the child's mother was given a letter addressed to the general practitioner asking him to supervise any further treatment.

Eight days later, when the patient returned to the department, the two fingers that had been strapped were found to be grossly discoloured, and partial amputation of each subsequently became necessary. The solicitor's letter alleging negligence preceded the amputations.

In forwarding the X-ray films to the protection society the legal adviser to the regional hospital board commented that the fracture must probably be a minor one for he was not sure that his 'untutored eye' had detected it. Examination of the films by many tutored eyes showed that the fracture did not in fact exist, and it was evident that the claim could not be contested.

Proportionate liability proved somewhat more difficult. Should a casualty officer supervise a staff nurse strapping a child's fingers, and should he inspect the strapping after its application? Should a staff nurse know that the ends of fingers should always be left exposed? Should the hospital authority have seen that a card with instructions regarding the need to watch the circulation was handed to patients who had had strapping applied as it was to patients with limbs or digits in plaster? What about the general practitioner? The patient attended his surgery a few hours after the fingers were strapped at the hospital. He had asked whether they were painful, and assuming from the answer that they were moderately so, had prescribed an analgesic. Should he have removed the strapping, or at least uncovered the ends of the fingers? Should he have instructed the mother to bring the child back the next morning?

And what of the parents? Not for eight days did they have the strapping removed or seek further medical advice. Was there failure to mitigate damages here? If there was thought to be such failure, could it possibly be pleaded in court when there had been no fracture in the first place?

Opinions on all these questions will vary widely, for they do not permit of any degree of certainty. In practice, however, agreements must be reached and settlement was achieved, the protection society accepting 50 per cent on behalf of the casualty officer and the regional hospital board, and the general practitioner's defence union contributing 25 per cent each.

A doctor was sued in respect of his failure to diagnose kernicterus. A diagnosis of physiological jaundice was made, based on an incorrect laboratory report that the infant's Rh factor was negative. It was apparent from the mother's records that she had a positive

Coombs' test, and the court's view was expressed as follows:

> 'No Van den Bergh's test which would prove the presence of bile in the brain was given and no follow-up haemoglobin test was ordered in spite of the fact that the second blood count made on the 6th November (4 days after birth) showed a significant drop in the haemoglobin, admittedly diagnostic evidence of the presence of erythroblastosis foetalis. . . . The testimony of various doctors established that a child of an Rh positive homozygous father and a sensitized Rh negative mother would be Rh positive, and in all probability suffer from erythroblastosis foetalis at birth. This medical testimony also showed that where laboratory tests are inconsistent with clinical findings the laboratory tests should be re-run, particularly in the circumstances of this case where a laboratory test, obviously wrong, showed the child as Rh negative. The medical evidence also showed that where a child of an Rh positive homozygous father and an Rh negative mother developed jaundice in the first few days of life, a Van den Bergh's test was strongly indicated. This same evidence showed that good medical practice would require a follow-up haemoglobin test in the circumstances of this case where the second haemoglobin test taken showed a falling blood count. The medical evidence also established that if the proper tests used in this area in 1953 had been run and re-run where indicated, a diagnosis of pathological, as distinguished from physiological, jaundice would have been required. The recognised treatment for pathological jaundice in this area was in 1953 and is now an exchange transfusion in which the blood of the baby is replaced with healthy blood. While the incidence of mortality in such operations was in 1953 10%, the alternative is paralysing brain damage and early death, and the recognised medical practice at that time, as now, was to undertake the exchange transfusion.'

The trial court found for the plaintiff and on appeal the decision of the trial court was confirmed.

A patient was admitted to hospital for a gastroscopic examination for the detection of possible cancer. The gastroscope was passed easily until the cardia was reached, when there appeared to be some spasm preventing further progress. The surgeon applied pressure and insufflation but surgical emphysema appeared and the patient showed signs of distress, whereupon the surgeon immediately suspected damage to the oesophageal wall and removed the gastroscope. A thoracotomy was undertaken and a tear about 1 inch in length was found and repaired.

The patient sued in negligence, producing no medical evidence other than that of the defendant surgeon himself. The court found for the defendant and the plaintiff appealed. The Supreme Court of Pennsylvania sustained the decision of the lower court, holding that where the patient did not offer expert medical testimony to prove that the defendant had manipulated the gastroscope improperly or had done anything else contrary to standard practice, the patient had no claim to damages.[2]

2. *Robinson* v. *Wirts*. Supreme Court of Pennsylvania. No. 387. Pa.St.291, 127A, 2d, 706.

4. Negligence in Treatment

The review of 500 chronological cases of alleged medical negligence referred to in the last chapter showed that, as regards treatment, the most common incidents concerned retained swabs, burns, anaesthetic accidents, the wrong operation and retained instruments.

There is, however, no possibility of classifying all the errors that can be made, and while the common misfortunes will undoubtedly be repeated in the future, at the same time new categories will equally certainly appear in endless variety. Without further preamble this chapter will detail cases concerned with treatment from the files of the Medical Protection Society.

Swabs, Instruments, and Drains

A patient was admitted to hospital as an emergency in the thirty-third week of pregnancy. Her blood pressure was 200/125, and continued to rise, reaching 240/150 three days later. The fundi were examined, both of which showed early retinal oedema and there was a small retinal haemorrhage in the right eye. Since medical treatment failed, a classical Caesarean section was performed. In spite of her grave condition the patient made an uneventful recovery from the operation but the infant had a marked spina bifida with paraplegia and died a few days later. When discharged the patient was asked to attend the post-natal clinic but did not do so, although on her return home she consulted her own doctor about severe abdominal pain for which she was ultimately admitted four months later to another hospital, where she subsequently died.

During her six weeks in this second hospital her condition appeared to improve at first, and she had no abdominal tenderness. Later, she developed urinary symptoms and diarrhoea, thought to be due to colitis. At autopsy the stomach was found markedly dilated. On palpation of the distended bowels a hard mass was noted and upon the bowel being opened this mass was found to be a gauze swab which, among other things, contained old food debris. The swab found was not of the type used at this second hospital. A professor of forensic medicine gave it as his opinion that the swab did not cause the disease from which the patient died and that there was no evidence that would justify his saying it had accelerated death.

Five months later, the widower, as administrator of his late wife's estate, instituted proceedings against the appropriate hospital management committee and the surgeon, claiming damages under the Fatal Accidents Acts and the Law Reform (Miscellaneous Provisions) Act for the loss of expectation of life. He alleged that the surgeon was negligent in that he left, or permitted to be left, during the Caesarean operation, a surgical swab. Because of the difficulties in this case in regard to the checking of swabs it was deemed advisable, in consultation with the solicitors to the hospital management committee, to arrive at a settlement, and in view of the fact that the patient's expectation of life had been poor a small sum was paid into the court and was accepted.

A consultant surgeon visited an elderly patient in his home. The patient was suffering from abdominal pain and was deeply jaundiced, and his symptoms were thought to be due most probably to gall stones, a diagnosis that was confirmed at the hospital to which he was subsequently admitted. After a few days in hospital the surgeon decided to remove the gall bladder and explore the bile ducts, although the patient was crippled with osteo-arthritis, had a raised blood pressure, and signs of cardiac weakness. The operation was the second on the surgeon's list, and during the first, which was very protracted, his house surgeon felt unwell and had to leave the theatre. A male theatre superintendent who had been acting as instrument nurse assisted for the remainder of the operation and another nurse 'scrubbed up' to attend to the instruments. At the second operation the surgeon was again assisted by the male theatre superintendent. The operation proceeded satisfactorily and the inexperience of the nurse in charge of the instruments caused no difficulties. However, at the end of the operation, as the surgeon was putting in the last skin suture, the theatre superintendent informed him that a pair of forceps was missing. He considered the alternatives of reopening the wound at once or of having an X-ray examination first to confirm that the missing forceps were in the abdomen, and he adopted the second course because he thought it best to confirm the presence of the forceps rather than prolong the operation. On the afternoon of the same day radiography revealed that the forceps were in the abdomen and he therefore re-opened the wound shortly afterwards. This operation was very brief, lasting about fifteen minutes, and the patient's condition was reasonably good throughout, but as a precaution he was given a blood transfusion. The next morning his condition had greatly deteriorated with symptoms of cardiac failure. A physician gave an opinion that he was suffering from left ventricular failure consequent upon high blood pressure. He died shortly afterwards, and at the inquest the cause of death was given as heart failure, but the Coroner thought that death had been accelerated by the operations and returned a verdict of death by misadventure.

A few days after the inquest the widow consulted solicitors who made a claim against the hospital management committee, and although the surgeon acted conscientiously and in the best interests of the patient throughout, it was agreed that a settlement was advisable, and that the society would contribute 50 per cent.

An exploratory operation was performed on a patient with a hydronephrotic left kidney. No renal calculus was found, so the wound was drained and after several weeks the patient was discharged. Shortly afterwards the wound broke down, necessitating his readmission, and when investigation showed that the function of the left kidney had further deteriorated, the surgeon decided to remove it. The operation was difficult because of induration and scar tissue but the patient made a speedy recovery and after ten days the wound was healed.

A year later the surgeon received a letter from solicitors alleging that a broken surgical needle had been removed by a doctor from their client's nephrectomy wound, and claiming damages. The society considered it was essential that the surgeon should, if possible, inspect the piece of needle, and this was arranged. He reported that it was the distal (pointed) 3 cm of a curved cutting needle not of a type he ordinarily used and that it could not have been broken by him because he would have been bound to have noticed it. He was equally certain that the needle could not have been left in the wound at the time of the first operation, because it would have been clearly visible on the X-ray films taken both after that operation and immediately prior to the second operation. How in the circumstances the needle came to be found in the wound was a mystery, but the surgeon suggested it might have been broken by one of the theatre staff when she was threading it and then placed on a swab to be thrown away later, but that either he or his assistant had inadvertantly picked up this swab and used it to staunch some bleeding, thus conveying the needle fragment into the wound.

Whatever the explanation of this curious accident, it was clear that the presence of the needle in the wound seven months after the operation could not be disputed and that the court would almost certainly find that somebody had been negligent. It was therefore decided that a settlement should be negotiated in collaboration with the hospital authority, who had also received notice of the claim from the patient's solicitors. The actual damage suffered by the patient was not great and he ultimately accepted a very modest sum of which the protection society paid one quarter.

A patient four months pregnant was seized with severe pain in the left iliac fossa, which her doctor diagnosed as due to a ruptured tubal pregnancy. Her admission to the nearest hospital involved travelling a considerable distance so that, despite an immediate blood transfusion on arrival, she was too ill to be moved from the ward to the operating theatre; the surgeon therefore decided he must use the ward bed as an operating table. When he opened the abdomen he found it full of blood and the uterus split vertically across the fundus. He ligatured bleeding vessels and repaired the damage while blood transfusion was continued. Before closing the abdomen, he confirmed by searching the theatre sister's statement that the swab count was correct. Subsequent recovery was complicated by ileus which, however, was successfully treated by gastric suction and intravenous therapy. Ten days later the patient had a mild attack of jaundice but was able to leave hospital apparently well after a stay of four weeks.

The surgeon heard nothing further until he received from the patient's husband a letter demanding compensation because his wife, after suffering much pain for several months, had a second operation at which a swab was found in her abdomen.

Attempts to prevent the action going into Court proved fruitless as the patient's solicitors refused to consider any sum less than £10,000 in settlement. The claim was therefore resisted, and at the trial, which lasted for 13 days, judgment was given jointly against the surgeon and the hospital for £2,500. The appelate court reversed the earlier judgment against the surgeon but dismissed the hospital's appeal, though it reduced the general damages awarded from £2,500 to £750. The court held that the Judge had failed entirely to appreciate that the patient was in a state of collapse during the whole of the operation and the improvement in her condition which followed the arrest of the bleeding only indicated that she was no longer actually dying but might possibly survive. The evidence was that the surgeon before sewing up had made both a visual and tactile search; that it would have been bad surgical practice and probably fatal to the patient to carry out a general search of the abdominal cavity; that he made and relied on his own mental count of the restraining packs and was under no duty to memorise the mopping packs; and that he relied on the theatre sister's count and she was someone of whose efficiency he had good reason to be confident.

A patient was admitted with a carcinoma of the breast, and mastectomy was performed. Rubber drains were inserted and secured by a safety pin and stitch. The house surgeon noted Post-operative condition satisfactory' two days later, and the day after that, when he himself saw the patient for the last time, 'Blood-stained discharge from wound, otherwise NAD'. Subsequently the patient was transferred to a continuation hospital before being discharged two weeks after the operation. A month after this the general practitioner removed a corrugated rubber drain about 6 inches long from the operation site, and three months later a further short piece of drain.

The usual practice at the hospital was that such drains were shortened on the second day and removed on the third, a task undertaken by the nursing staff and recorded on the charts. It was the duty of the medical staff to inspect the wound before transfer to the continuation hospital, or discharge, and at other times if necessary. In this case it was a fact that two portions of drain had been left in the wound, and since the oversight should not have occurred, it was clearly necessary to compensate the patient for anything that she had suffered as a result. Although the total amount was not likely to be very large, a more difficult question to be resolved was the proportions into which such a settlement should be divided between medical and nursing staff. It was not known exactly what had been recovered from the wound by the practitioner, for it was merely described as 'corrugated rubber drain', and there was no mention of the safety pin known to have been inserted at the time of the operation to prevent the drain from slipping back. It seemed likely, therefore, that the external portion into which the pin was attached had been removed when the drain was shortened by the nurse and that the pin had not been replaced. This would have allowed the drain to slip into the wound and be lost. The charts recorded 'drain shortened' on the second post-operative day but no further mention was made of shortening or removal, and this tended to confirm the supposition. After discussion, a 50/50 apportionment of responsibility with the hospital was agreed.

Whereas the vaginal tampon is hailed as a major contribution to hygiene, as soon as an equivalent swab is retained in the vagina by mistake it immediately becomes a potential cause for litigation, being blamed for a wide variety of symptoms. In this case the obstetrical house surgeon had performed a perineal repair, following an episiotomy during the delivery of twins. After a normal puerperium the patient was discharged on the ninth day but six weeks after delivery a gauze swab was recovered from the vagina by the general practitioner, this having undoubtedly remained *in situ* since the perineal repair.

A short while later a solicitor's letter was received setting out the details of damage the patient was alleged to have sustained as a result of this oversight, including the allegation that while the foreign body was in position, she was unable to stand on her feet for very long and could only walk for short distances. She complained of pains in her stomach and stated that she had not been able to look after her children as a result, and there was much else besides.

While it was considered very doubtful whether any such damage had actually been sustained, it was an undeniable fact that the swab had been left, and it might have resulted in some symptoms. It was therefore agreed that a settlement should be explored.

A thoracic surgeon performed decortication of a lung, and inserted two drainage tubes which, according to the notes, were removed three days later. The patient made a good recovery and returned to work though remaining under the surveillance of the chest physician.

Seventeen years after the operation the patient had a small haemoptysis. Radiography did not disclose any cause but two months later he suffered a further haemoptysis and died within a few hours. Post-mortem examination revealed an ulcerated sinus in the lung caused by a length of drainage tubing, and the haemorrhage had apparently occurred from this part of the lung. At the subsequent inquest the pathologist expressed the opinion that the deceased would have lived but for the presence of the tube. Some months later a claim was made against the regional hospital board. The Board sought the views of the society, whose first problem was created by the fact that the surgeon had predeceased the patient by some years. Investigation showed that the tube had torn at a point where a drainage hole had been cut in it, and in view of the length of time that had elapsed it was considered pointless to debate whether too large a hole had been cut by the surgeon or whether a nurse removing the tube should have been aware that a portion had been retained. The chest physician under whose care the patient had been gave his opinion that but for the tube he would have expected his patient to work up to normal retiring age, whereas in the event the deceased was only in his early forties at the time of his death.

Counsel's opinion was as to the effect that the court would find that the presence of the piece of tubing was adequate proof of negligence and he advised therefore that a settlement be negotiated. The deceased being a married man with children, the settlement was necessarily a substantial one, to which the society contributed 50 per cent on behalf of their late member. This was the second case to arise following this member's death. Both cases were indefensible and were settled without, to the best of the protection society's knowledge, his widow or family ever being aware that a claim had been made.

A middle-aged man weighing over 18 stone (252 lb) was admitted to a professorial medical unit with a provisional diagnosis of coronary thrombosis. The day after admission, however, it was thought that the trouble centered in the abdomen, a tentative diagnosis of intestinal obstruction was made, and the abdomen was opened by a surgical registrar. Some fat necrosis was found in the omentum, a diagnosis of acute pancreatitis was made, and the abdomen closed. The anaesthetist experienced some difficulty in re-establishing respiration, and shortly after the patient had fully recovered from the anaesthetic an artery forceps was reported to be missing. Search of the theatre proving negative, radiography by a portable X-ray machine revealed the errant forceps in the patient's abdomen. The following day the situation was carefully considered and it was decided to operate that evening to remove the forceps. At this time the result of a serum amylase estimation made its belated appearance on the ward. This test had, unbeknown to the surgical registrar, been ordered on the day of admission by the house physician and the amylase level very strongly suggested the correct diagnosis. In the absence of the chemical pathologist, his technician had not thought to telephone such a result through to the ward.

The operation to remove the forceps proceeded uneventfully, but shortly after its conclusion the patient collapsed and died. The surgical registrar then heard for the first time of a hospital rule introduced some while previously but never apparently brought specifically to his notice, to the effect that the hospital authority considered it impractical to count instruments after each operation and therefore relied upon surgeons taking extra care. A hospital enquiry dealt very reasonably with the matter, appreciating fully the difference between looking for forceps known to be missing and the routine examination of the abdomen of an 18-stone patient to check that nothing had been left behind.

When a claim in negligence was subsequently made difficulties arose between the hospital authority and the society in that the former took the view that their rule placed the major share of the responsibility on the registrar whereas the society considered that the abandonment of the routine instrument count was the essential cause of the mishap. Eventually agreement was reached to share the liability equally.

Protracted negotiations regarding quantum ensued. Here was an obese middle-aged man whose general health was far from good, suffering from a condition which carried a substantial mortality and which might in any event have recurred. On the other hand, he had, though a poor surgical risk, survived the first operation; the pancreatitis was, it seemed, not particularly severe, and there was a reasonable prospect that he might have continued in his Trade Union post until retiring age. The Union solicitors put in a claim so far above what was thought to be reasonable that for a period it looked as though the matter might have to go to court purely on the question of quantum. Finally, almost two years after the patient's death, agreement was reached and a sum considered by both sides to be equitable was paid to the patient's widow.

Some four to five months following a colostomy a patient complained of bleeding from the ostium, and when the surgeon

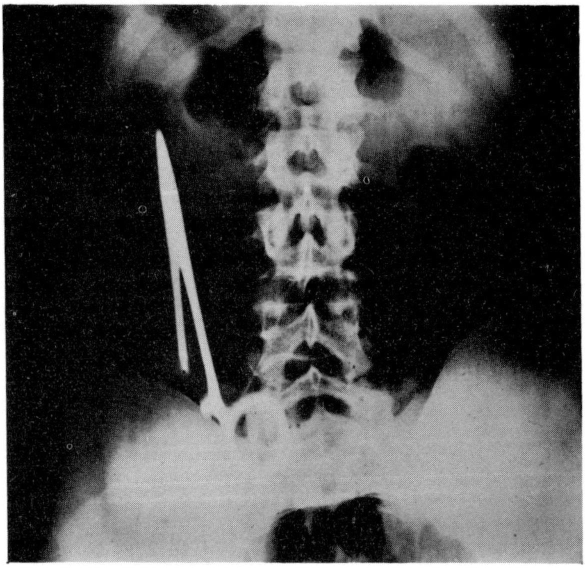

Fig. 15

inserted his finger he was horrified to withdraw that part of the Spencer Wells not illustrated in Fig. 15.

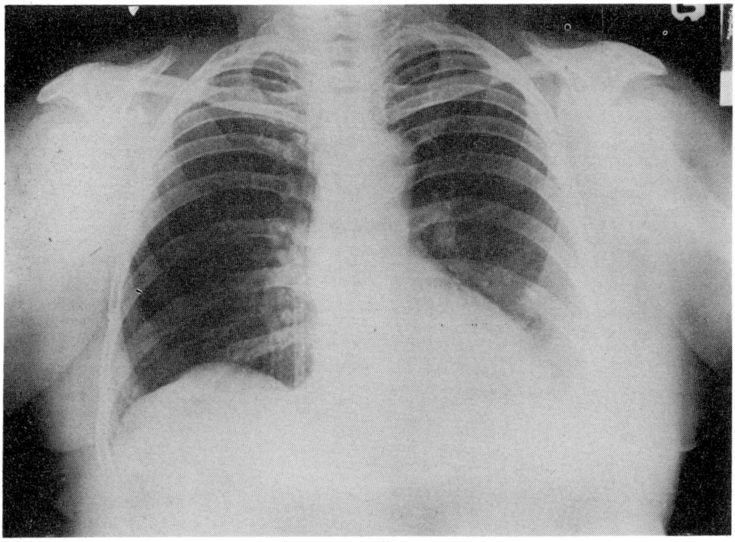

Fig. 16

A patient had a radical mastectomy following which she continued to complain of discomfort which she located over the sternum. Sternal secondaries were feared, and a large series of X-rays were taken but it was not until three years after the operation that the tube shown in Fig. 16 was observed.

A paracentesis was carried out on a patient with hydramnios.

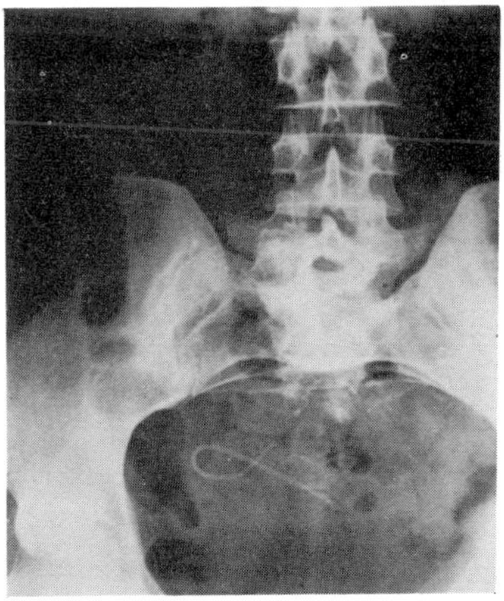

Fig. 17

Some eighteen months later an X-ray of the abdomen was taken and part of the catheter used for the paracentesis was found to have remained *in situ* (Fig. 17).

Burns

A general practitioner who held a part-time appointment at the local hospital was requested to see a patient who attended as a casualty suffering from epistaxis. The doctor asked the sister for some adrenalin, his intention being to plug the nose with gauze soaked in this solution. The sister went to the theatre and returned with a bottle but did not hand this to the doctor. She was about to dip the gauze in the bottle when an orderly came in with another bottle and made some remark to the sister to the effect that the ENT specialist used the particular substance in this second bottle for epistaxis cases; he thereupon handed the second bottle to her. The doctor did not look at it and assumed it contained adrenalin chloride and a coagulant. The sister dipped a plug of gauze into the second bottle and handed it to the doctor who got it as far as the anterior nares of the patient when it was immediately seen that the patient's moustache and the side of his nose were turning white. The gauze was removed and the nose itself was never actually plugged, for the doctor realised at once that something was wrong and on looking at this second bottle found that it contained trichloracetic acid. He at once neutralised the acid application by using an alkaline solution, but considerable damage resulted.

The patient consulted solicitors who threatened proceedings against the hospital management committee concerned and the doctor. A surgeon examined the patient on behalf of the protection society and in view of his report it was thought advisable to explore a settlement, which was eventually brought about successfully.

A patient was admitted to a hospital in Northern Ireland suffering from very advanced degenerative arthritis in her left knee-joint which was becoming worse. Six months later she was referred to the orthopaedic department, where it was confirmed that she had advanced osteo-arthritis in the left knee-joint but the orthopaedic surgeon advised against operation because the patient was very obese and not likely to be a good subject. The patient was not satisfied with this opinion and therefore consulted another surgeon in the hospital. He aspirated the left knee-joint and found it full of thick fluid. This, however, did not help the condition and the patient was informed that the only chance of relieving this would be to open the joint, excise all the diseased and inflammatory tissue, and remove the cartilage from the end of the bones, thus producing a fixed but painless joint. Some weeks later excision and arthrodesis were performed but while the limb was subsequently being encased in paster of Paris it was noticed that the patient was suffering from a severe degree of surgical shock. An intravenous drip of glucose saline was started and later a blood transfusion was given. In addition, when she returned to bed, heat treatment by means of an electric cradle was given. The next morning she was considerably improved but it was found that her abdomen and the upper part of her thighs had been burned, presumably by the heat cradle. The patient's condition slowly improved, and the burns on the abdomen and thighs for the most part gradually healed but there remained an area of the abdominal wall that had to be excised, and some areas required skin grafting.

Later the patient brought an action against the management committee of the hospital. After full consideration the conclusion was reached that although the patient was covered with a blanket, steps should have been taken to ensure that the lamps in the cradle were located at a safe distance from her body, which in fact they were not by reason of her inordinate size. Ultimately the action was settled by the insurers of the hospital, the protection society, acting on behalf of the doctor who had placed the cradle in position, contributing to the sum paid.

A married woman entered hospital for laparotomy and cauterisation of the cervix uteri. After the abdominal operation she was placed in the lithotomy position and the vagina was swabbed out with Cetavlon, followed by spirit, the same routine having been followed earlier when the skin of the abdomen was sterilised. A speculum was placed in position and the cervix seized with a volsellum but when the operator approximated the diathermy electrode to the vulva there was a spark and momentary flash of flame. A few seconds later it was noticed that the towel folds around the patient's buttocks were markedly hot, and when the patient was turned over it was realised that the excess spirit used in the earlier skin preparation had run down the patient's flanks and soaked into the towels beneath her buttocks which were extensively burned in a butterfly-shaped area. Subsequently two skin-grafting operations were required, and some five weeks after the original operation she was discharged with very tender buttocks on which she was unable to sit for any length of time.

A claim followed, and a consultant surgeon reported ten months after the accident that she was still complaining of nerves, fits of depression and insomnia, and that she had pain in the buttocks and right hip, was unable to sit for long and had an aching sensation in the sacral area. He found the grafted area well covered and the skin supple and mobile with minimal scarring and no keloid formation. In his opinion the result was first class and there was no reason why the patient should suffer permanent disability. He considered her present complaints were largely inconsistent with his physical findings and the origin of some of them was functional rather than organic.

The plaintiff had formulated a claim for £1,500 but later agreed to accept a much smaller sum.

In 1957 a patient was admitted to hospital for a minor gynaecological operation which was performed by a locum registrar. Before the operation, the necessary instruments were sterilized by boiling and placed on a sterile trolley, and cold sterile water was available in a bowl on an adjacent stand. Neither the operator nor any other person present in the theatre was aware of anything untoward having occurred during the operation but subsequently the patient was found to have a burn on her right buttock measuring 3 by 2 inches, apparently caused by a speculum. Before this healed, skin-grafting was necessary, so that the patient had to remain in hospital six weeks instead of just a few days. Although a claim was made against the hospital concerned within six months of the occurrence, reliable information about the accident proved difficult to obtain. The registrar who performed the operation was considered by the hospital authorities to have been responsible but he apparently left his locum tenens post without any knowledge of the burn he was alleged to have caused. When the society requested a detailed report he replied from overseas that he had no recollection of any accidental burn to a patient and was quite sure that he was in no way to blame. A further difficulty was that the consultant under whose care the patient had been admitted went on holiday after the operation and was never informed of the burn nor had she seen it.

After receipt of the particulars of claim the hospital obtained a report on the patient's present condition. Examination confirmed the presence of a well-healed scar on the buttock measuring 2½ by 1½ inches which had been treated by a skin graft, and the hospital admitted that this graft was applied while she was an in-patient subsequent to the gynaecological operation.

Although it was thought difficult to believe that the registrar would not have noticed the injury to the buttock at the time of the operation, if indeed it occurred then, the patient clearly had a sound claim and it was agreed that a settlement should be effected by the hospital solicitors and that the protection society would contribute towards it.

A six-year-old boy with epistaxis was taken to see an ENT surgeon in the Middle East. Examination revealed bleeding points in both nostrils and it was proposed to cauterize these with trichloracetic acid after anaesthetising the area. Soaked pledgets of cotton wool were therefore placed in position and the parents instructed to wait for ten minutes. On their return the surgeon searched for the trichloracetic acid and then realised that he had in fact used it in error for cocaine. He later explained that it was his habit to keep these and other solutions in glass bottles in a wooden box and he was careful to keep each bottle in a definite position. On this occasion his nurse had been cleaning out the box and had replaced the bottles incorrectly. The boy suffered scarring which resulted in his having to be brought to England for skin grafting, and in due course solicitors were instructed and lodged a claim on his behalf. The matter was clearly indefensible and a settlement was achieved under which the protection society met the total expenses and costs.

A house surgeon used trichloracetic acid to cauterize the nose of a young woman suffering from epistaxis. Whereas there was dispute as to whether the patient sneezed, undoubtedly some of the acid ran on to her upper lip, and despite the application of sodium bicarbonate, some scarring resulted.

It was alleged that the member had been negligent in permitting the acid to drop on to the patient's lip and in failing to take sufficient measures to avoid injury, and furthermore that the maxim *res ipsa loquitur* applied. The injuries were said to consist of chemical burns of the left nostril and lip, scarring inside the nostril causing narrowing, and a vertical scar on the upper lip $\frac{1}{2}$ inch long by $\frac{1}{8}$ inch wide raised $\frac{1}{16}$ inch above the surface of the skin. These injuries were substantially agreed but there were quite unacceptable allegations that the acid had caused deflection of the nasal septum.

On behalf of the society the patient was examined by an eminent dermatologist who agreed the injuries referred to above, adding that 'without exaggeration she cannot be described as good looking.' An ENT surgeon was then approached for his views on the house surgeon's technique. He reported that the patient's sneeze, which the house surgeon said caused the acid to run from the nostril, could suggest inadequate anaesthesia, and that this was supported by the fact that a spray rather than prolonged surface application or submucous injection was used. Futhermore, he felt that the extent of the burns could only be accounted for by the use of an excessive amount of the trichloracetic acid. It was therefore decided to explore a settlement, and while the protection society's experts felt that plastic procedures were not indicated, the patient had meanwhile consulted a practitioner who in his assessment of the damages included a substantial amount to cover the cost of plastic surgery which he advised might be required. As the possibility could not be denied that the patient might at some future date undergo such an operative procedure a fairly substantial sum was paid in settlement.

Trichloracetic acid was being used as a cauterising agent when the pledget fell from the probe on to the patient's chin, resulting in a 4 inch linear keloid scar running from the point of the chin down the anterior line of the neck (Fig. 18). As it could not be thought that a pledget correctly applied would fall from a probe nor that the quantity of acid required for cauterisation would cause such an extensive scar, a settlement had to be negotiated.

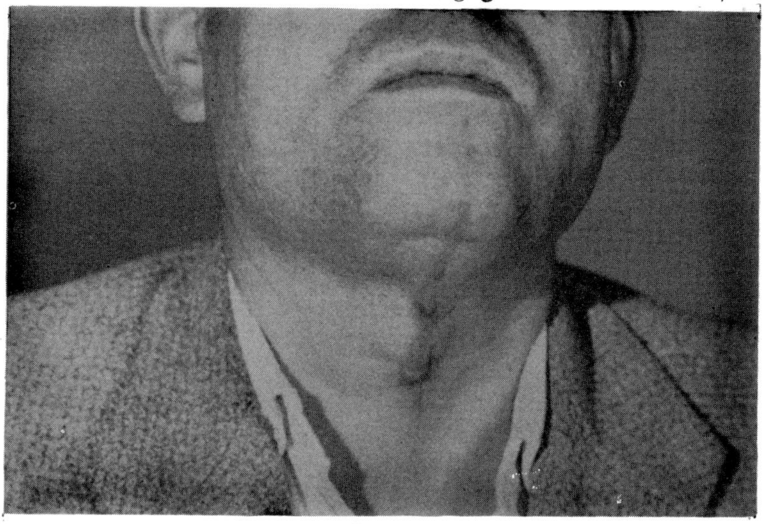

Fig. 18

A registrar who had considerable experience overseas circumcised a six-month old baby. He used tissue crushing forceps, removed the prepuce distal to the forceps with fine scissors, and applied a diathermy electrode to secure haemostasis. As a result the child suffered a burn of the skin of the penis, and the following day the injury was described as 'a deep localised burn involving half the circumference of the penis at the peno-scrotal junction ventrally. In addition the viability of the skin over the distal half of the shaft of the penis appeared doubtful.' Eight days later a plastic surgeon removed 'all the white burned epithelium of the penile shaft'. He further reported that 'underneath, the deeper tissues looked white in places and were not viable enough to take a split skin graft. A catheter was passed easily but it was seen that there was only a very thin layer of tissue covering the undersurface of the urethra and parts of this were grey in colour . . .' Soon after this the urethra at the peno-scrotal junction broke away, a fistula developed, and the penile shaft and glans sloughed away. Six weeks later there appeared to be a total loss of all the visible shaft of the penis but the plastic surgeon thought about 30 per cent of the corpora cavernosa had survived. He gave a guarded prognosis and referred to the problem of reconstruction as very great, if not impossible.

When the case was considered by the society it was agreed that the current from the diathermy electrode must have passed through the bone forceps to all the tissues of the penis and as it was held well away from the baby's body, it constituted the narrowest part of the electric circuit, hence the serious damage. Agreement was reached with the hospital authorities that any claim that might arise would be indefensible and to any settlement negotiated they agreed to contribute 10 per cent. At first it was feared that, in view of the surgeon's grave prognosis, this sum might reach five figures, but when, three years after the operation, negotiations were started, the society were pleased to learn that the child's condition had improved beyond all expectations. A surgeon who had seen the child from time to time since the accident was able to report that urinary function was almost normal except for a narrow stream and that the 'injuries he had sustained would not prevent him from becoming a father'. In the circumstances Counsel for the parents advised their acceptance of a sum only a fraction of the original estimate. This settlement (as the law requires in the case of infants) was shortly afterwards approved by a Judge of the High Court.

A barman in South Africa suffering from penile warts, which treatment by a dermatologist had failed to remove, was referred to a radiotherapist. A course of treatment of eight sessions was given, covering three areas, each of which contained approximately ten warts. Unfortunately, when the patient was seen two months later the warts were still present and the course was therefore repeated. This disposed of the warts, but subsequently ulceration of the penis developed, involving the whole circumference, and led to the patient undergoing three plastic operations. The final result was that the penis was shortened and rotated, very little of the corpora cavernosa was left, sexual intercourse was possible only with considerable difficulty, and a perineal urethrostomy had been necessary. In brief, the penis was described as having an 85 per cent loss of function.

Some two years after the treatment complained of, the radiologist received a solicitor's letter alleging negligence and demanding the equivalent of £75,000. One expert considered the dose too high, another was prepared to support the total dose given but considered that the interval between the courses was too short, a third held that while the treatment was not unreasonable he would not himself have given it.

The Writ and Statement of Claim came in due course, the claim now being reduced to £20,000. The question of contributory negligence on the patient's part was canvassed. He had, for example, been an irregular attender for treatment, had failed to keep the part clean, and, according to the member, had admitted to having sexual intercourse shortly after the therapy had been completed, though asked to abstain. On the other hand, it might be questioned whether it was reasonable, given that type of patient, to advocate a treatment the success of which was dependent upon a standard of cleanliness and self-control foreign to his nature.

Other expert opinions were obtained and the patient was further examined by a genito-urinary surgeon and a radiotherapist. Eventually a position was reached where every part of the member's treatment of the case was supported by at least one expert, but not one would go the whole way with him. Thus, none, if asked in the witness box 'Would you have given similar treatment?', could have given an unqualified affirmative. In such circumstances the outcome was uncertain and a trial of such an issue would inevitably be prolonged and be widely reported, with consequent potential harm to the member's practice.

Finally, the plaintiff's attorney's called for a pre-trial conference in accordance with the Rules of Court in South Africa, and the opportunity was taken by the Society's solicitors' agents of sounding them as to the possibility of a settlement out of court. This was ultimately agreed at a payment of a much more moderate sum without admission of liability.

A young married woman was admitted to hospital for tonsillectomy. The operation was performed by a senior house officer assisted by a student nurse. At the close of the operation, which had been performed without incident, bilateral superficial burns were seen on the sides of the neck in positions which corresponded to those of the suspension rods used to support the mouth gag (Fig. 19). Neither the surgeon nor the nurse had been able to feel the heat of the rods through their gloves.

The burns healed but the residual scarring remained, easily

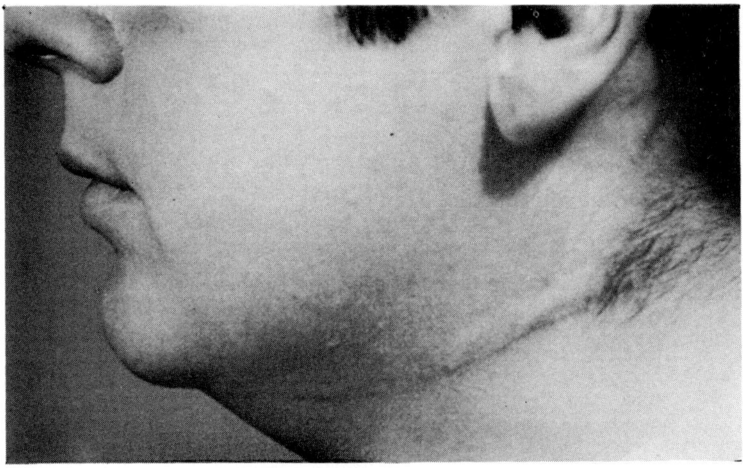

Fig. 19

noticeable and of a permanent nature. The patient subsequently made a claim for damages which could not be resisted.

Anaesthetics

A patient suffering from a pilonidal sinus consulted her doctor, who sent her to the local hospital where she was advised that a minor operation was necessary.

Five months later she was admitted to hospital for operation and it was arranged that a general practitioner, who was a part-time anaesthetist, should give her the anaesthetic. On the day of the operation there were three cases in all for the doctor to anaesthetise. The first two were children, who were anaesthetised without difficulty. The adult patient after premedication with omnopon and scopolamine was given intravenous thiopentone and an intra-tracheal tube was passed. As the doctor did not wish to give the same mixture of gases as he had just used for the children, certain alterations in the assembly of the tubes was necessary. Unfortunately, when reconnecting the apparatus he picked up the open end of a tube which he mistakenly thought came from the gas flow-meters when in fact it was the other free end of a long tube that had been left on the anaesthetic trolley following a tonsillectomy operation the previous day. This resulted in the patient receiving neither anaesthetic gases nor oxygen since she was merely breathing atmospheric air through the long tube.

Just as the patient was being turned over it was noticed that respiration had ceased and the pulse could not be felt. The doctor therefore turned on the oxygen to full pressure but, of course, none reached the patient. When he discovered this he immediately disconnected the apparatus and tried artificial respiration and other restorative measures, but with no effect.

The death was reported to the Coroner and at the inquest it was stated that the cause of death was pulmonary collapse and anoxia which occurred at the conclusion of an operation for the excision of a pilonidal sinus, and that the said anoxia followed the faulty connection of the apparatus used for the administration of the anaesthetic, and a verdict of death by misadventure was returned.

Following the inquest the husband consulted solicitors who made a claim against the doctor for damages under the Law Reform (Miscellaneous Provisions) Act and under the Fatal Accidents Act. In regard to the claim under the Fatal Accidents Act, the widower alleged that he was partially dependent on his late wife as was his wife's mother.

When the case was considered it was deemed right and proper to admit the doctor's liability because it was he who had made the mistake in assembling the apparatus. The plaintiff's claim, however, was so greatly exaggerated that it was impossible to arrive at an equitable settlement. It therefore became necessary to defend the proceedings in respect of the quantum of damages claimed but a sum of money paid into court prior to the trial was ultimately accepted.

A doctor who, though qualified for several years, was occupying the position of a house surgeon, was entrusted to carry out a submucous resection and tonsillectomy. Progress was somewhat slow as the resection took one and a half hours, and then removal of the right tonsil was started. Finding that the endotracheal tube hampered him, the house surgeon removed it, but the anaesthetic registrar felt it necessary to replace it a few moments later. When replaced, the tube was held in position by the gag and sterile towelling but was no longer strapped. The tonsil was found to be very adherent, so the consultant surgeon was summoned and completed its removal, demonstrating to the house surgeon his technique for dealing with this problem. The consultant was then quite satisfied with the patient's condition and with his houseman's ability to complete the operation, and indeed felt that had he remained, his presence could only have had an unsettling effect. The registrar anaesthetist had by this time been replaced by a senior house officer anaesthetist. The removal of the left tonsil was then duly completed.

It was noticed simultaneously that the bag on the anaesthetic machine was not moving, and that the endotracheal tube had come out. The consultant was summoned, the tube replaced, and resuscitation attempted. Open cardiac massage was successful after some 40 minutes, tracheotomy was subsequently performed, but some hours later the patient's condition deteriorated and he died about nine hours after the termination of the operation.

An inquest followed, and subsequently claims alleging negligence were made against all the doctors concerned and the regional hospital board. Negotiations were very protracted and before they were completed both the house surgeon and the senior house officer had left the country. Regarding these two doctors it was felt that the court would consider the probability was that one or both of them should, if employing reasonable skill and care, have observed earlier that all was not well. This view, combined with the fact that both were abroad, necessitated the negotiation of a settlement which had to be effected for a very large sum.

A man of thirty was undergoing a ureterolithotomy, the anaesthetic being administered by a consultant anaesthetist. Anaesthesia for the operation, which lasted for 2 hours 45 minutes, was provided by nitrous oxide and oxygen, relaxation being secured by the injection of curare and pethidine. At the end of the operation Lethidrone and nikethamide were administered and the patient was returned to the ward. Before the patient left the theatre, the anaesthetist was satisfied with his condition, as he was then recovering consciousness and reacting to stimuli. He reached the ward a quarter of an hour after the completion of the operation and 55 minutes later his condition was recorded by the nursing staff as 'satisfactory'. However, about half an hour after this he was found to be collapsed and he died soon afterwards.

The matter was complicated by the fact that there was no proper recovery ward at this hospital and that representations had previously been made to the hospital authority with the possibility of such an occurrence as the present case in mind. It was argued, on the one hand, that in these circumstances an anaesthetist should remain with the patient until full recovery was established, and, on the other, that to carry out this counsel of perfection in every case would mean, in effect, that the normal work of the surgical side would be at best drastically curtailed if not indeed brought to a stop. It seemed most probable that the patient's death was due to respiratory obstruction, which, of course, should not have been allowed to occur, and that in the circumstances the claim on behalf of the relatives could not be defended. It was strongly argued that as the potentially dangerous state of affairs obtaining at the hospital had been repeatedly drawn to the attention of the administrators, the major responsibility was theirs, and it was eventually agreed that the settlement should be made on the basis of a 75 per cent contribution from the hospital and 25 per cent from the protection society on behalf of the anaesthetist.

Injections and Vaccinations

A part-time consultant in physical medicine at a London hospital saw a patient at the request of his general practitioner. The patient had been complaining for some considerable time of increasing uselessness of his hands, in particular the right hand. He was also asthmatic. A number of doctors and surgeons whom he had seen expressed different views as to the cause of his disability, which distressed him the more because he was a furrier and a radio mechanic and depended to a large extent on his hands for his work. After a very careful examination the consultant diagnosed a scalenus anticus syndrome secondary to osteo-arthritis of the cervical spine and associated with an anxiety neurosis and emphysema. Following this diagnosis he advised remedial treatment consisting of shoulder exercises and faradism, and this treatment was given at the patient's own home by a physiotherapist from the hospital. Two months later the consultant again saw the patient who, although agreeing that the hands were stronger, complained that the arm and forearm muscles were weak. Perseverance with the treatment was urged. About ten weeks later he again saw his patient and found that although there was less pain the hand was useless and the patient depressed. The consultant told the patient that in his opinion the trouble arose from an irritation of the nerve supply and interference with the

circulation of the hand caused by muscle spasm, and advised an injection to relax this. The patient agreed to have this treatment and the consultant forthwith injected into the right scalenus anticus muscle 2·5 ml of 2 per cent procaine. Immediately after the injection the patient, as expected, exhibited Horner's syndrome. One week later the consultant saw the patient again and learned that for three days he had been much better.
In view of this he decided to repeat the treatment and gave a second injection in precisely the same manner as the first. This, once more, was followed by the exhibition of Horner's syndrome but the patient also complained of pain and faintness and was advised to lie down. This he did, and was left in the charge of a physiotherapist while the consultant was out of the room for ten minutes. When he returned he found that the patient had gone home in spite of requests by the physiotherapist that he should stay. The next day the patient's doctor telephoned the consultant requesting a domiciliary visit when it was found that the patient had pain in the right chest and difficulty in breathing. He was thereupon admitted to the hospital with a provisional diagnosis of pneumothorax, and on investigation it was found that he had in fact a haemopneumothorax. He remained in hospital just over a month but attended the out-patient department for some considerable time afterwards.

While he was still attending as an out-patient he consulted solicitors and began proceedings against the consultant and the regional hospital board. In these proceedings the patient alleged that the consultant in the course of an injection punctured the lung and a blood vessel and created the haemopneumothorax. Liability was denied and the action finally went to trial which concluded with judgment being given for the consultant and the board, with costs.

For a number of years a general practitioner had been treating a female patient who suffered from an iron deficiency anaemia. He had previously prescribed various liver preparations and iron by mouth but decided to give her a course of intramuscular injections of an iron preparation.

He gave six injections at weekly intervals into the deltoid region of each arm but the patient complained of the discoloration of the skin over the injection sites before the course was completed. Two years later the staining was still present and the patient asked him to refer her to a consultant in the hope that some remedy for her disfigurement could be recommended. The dermatologist who saw her at first considered that he might be able to help her, but after inquiry the manufacturers of the preparation made it clear that whereas with the passage of time the discoloration would probably tend to disappear there was no way in which this could be hastened, nor any certainty as to how long the natural process of fading would take.

With some appearance of reluctance, the patient finally consulted a solicitor who wrote a reasonable letter on her behalf to the doctor. No claim for damages was mentioned but the purport of the letter was to the effect that the solicitor had been greatly shocked to learn that her disfigurement would not improve and accordingly expected some recompense from her doctor whose treatment had caused the condition.

By the time the case was undertaken by the protection society information had been received from the manufacturers which made it clear that a successful defence would be difficult if not impossible. It was stated that enclosed with each batch of ampoules there were clear directions that the substance should be injected only into the gluteal muscles in the upper and outer quadrant of the buttock and that special care should be used in actually making the injection so as to avoid the iron solution leaking back along the needle track into the superficial tissues.

The protection society's solicitors were accordingly instructed to negotiate a settlement.

In 1955, a baby boy developed infantile eczema when three weeks old. The condition varied from time to time, but when he was six months old a severe generalised exacerbation necessitated admission to hospital. Three weeks treatment produced improvement and during the subsequent quiescent phase the parents requested their family doctor to vaccinate him.

Two days after vaccination, because the baby became listless and appeared ill, his mother took him to their doctor's partner who was deputising for the former during his absence. Local application of calamine lotion was prescribed and continued, but blisters developed on the vaccinated arm and elsewhere, and the baby's general condition deteriorated. The parents in consequence were so concerned that they decided to call in a third doctor, who, after visiting daily for 12 days, arranged his admission to hospital.

On arrival there he was found to be very ill, and diagnosed as suffering from severe generalised vaccinia. Skin lesions, which became secondarily infected with streptococci, were described in the hospital notes as very extensive, and when he was discharged seven weeks later concern was expressed about the possibility of keloid formation in the scar tissue at the site of the vaccination. When seen after three weeks as an out-patient, his general condition was good but he had a recrudescence of his eczema and the dermatologist was of the opinion that two scars on the left arm had already become definitely keloidal. He wished to keep the case under close observation but at this stage the family moved out of the district.

The doctor heard no more of the matter until he received a solicitor's letter in February 1957, which gave notice of the father's intention to make a claim on behalf of his infant son against him, on the grounds that he was negligent in vaccinating a child known to suffer from infantile eczema.

In the following October a Writ and Statement of Claim were issued, but by this time the child was living in Germany where his father was serving in H.M. forces. On this account difficulties arose about having the child examined by an expert and this could not be arranged until early in 1958. The report obtained confirmed that the child had suffered from eczema since early infancy and as a result of the vaccination performed in 1955 had developed severe generalised vaccinia. At the time of his examination the dermatologist stated that the child had on its left arm an extensive scar, resembling that from a scald, extending from the insertion of the deltoid muscle almost to the wrist; in addition, there were discrete superficial scars elsewhere all over the trunk, head, and limbs. These included scars on the lips and in front of the ears which he advised would persist and constitute a permanent cosmetic disability. As to the large scar on the left arm, although this in parts was hypertrophied, it was not in his opinion keloidal and there was no functional disability.

Liability was not contested but negotiations were protracted as no less than £5,000 was claimed. In the event, a payment into court of little more than one-tenth of this amount was accepted and approved by the court.

A general practitioner, consulted by a professional singer with an acute attack of gout, was asked for treatment as a temporary resident under the National Health Service. The patient stated that he had found that intravenous colchicine helped his gout and handed the doctor an ampoule containing 3 mg which he asked him to inject. The injection was started but the patient complained of pain and the needle was withdrawn, less than a quarter of the solution having been used. The following day the patient still complained of pain in the arm but did not blame the member at that time.

Three months later the doctor received a letter from the patient's solicitors stating that, in consequence of negligence in carrying out the injection, the patient had been and still was in great pain, and was unable to fulfil his professional engagements. The opinion of a neurologist was obtained and this confirmed that the patient was suffering from severe causalgia of median nerve distribution almost certainly caused by colchicine, which is known to be extremely irritant if injected extravenously, and on Counsel's advice a moderate sum was paid into court without admission of liability. In his answers to direct questions, the doctor stated that he did not know that colchicine was an irritant as he did not normally use it intravenously and indeed had only done so on this occasion at the request of the patient, and furthermore that he had not checked that the needle was in the vein by withdrawing blood into the syringe.

In view of these admissions it was clear that liability could not be denied and the action could be contested only on the quantum of damages. It was now two years since the accident occurred and a further report from the neurologist revealed that the condition had not improved as he had hoped – the skin of the hand was still very tender, use of the fingers restricted, the hand often very cold, and novocaine injection of the stellate ganglion had not helped. The prognosis was felt to be very poor.

On receipt of this report the amount paid into court was substantially increased and after some further months of negotiation settlement was eventually reached.

A laboratory assistant, while using a grinding wheel, omitted to wear protective goggles and shortly afterwards attended his general practitioner who removed a foreign body from his left cornea. Three days later the general practitioner removed a second foreign body, and four days after that the patient attended again, this time with severe inflammation of the eye. The next patient but one to see the doctor during that surgery was a child whom he had vaccinated four days previously. He then noticed that his vaccination needle was missing from its cork and that an extra needle was present in a cupboard. Realising that he might have vaccinated the cornea, the practitioner referred his patient for consultant advice.

The ophthalmologist diagnosed two corneal ulcers which he felt might be traumatic, but later a virus keratitis became apparent. Herpes simplex was first thought to be the cause but an amended report from the virologist confirmed the isolation of vaccinial virus.

The patient's employer then consulted the general practitioner about the eye, in the latter's role of Industrial Health Advisor to the firm. He stressed the employee's failure to wear protective goggles supplied, and the practitioner told him that the infection could have been contracted in his surgery.

Subsequently the patient had a corneal graft, the ophthalmologist reported to the patient's solicitors that the infection rather than the original injury was the essential cause of the patient's disability, the practitioner emigrated, and a Writ was issued against the partnership.

It was apparent that the sequence of events could not be defended and that a settlement must needs be explored. The patient's solicitors were therefore asked not to serve the Writ and given the necessary assurances to enable them to take this course. The remaining partners were informed that they would in no way become involved, and a settlement was negotiated.

Medicaments

A young man, suffering from extensive bilateral pulmonary tuberculosis, was admitted to hospital. After three weeks he appeared to be improving, but complained of inability to sleep so the doctor gave instructions that he should be given paraldehyde in water as a sedative at night. When this was administered he immediately said 'It's burnt me, Sister', spat it out, and retched. Later he drank some milk and slept reasonably well for the remainder of the night.

The facts were reported to the day sister who examined his throat, but could see no evidence of soreness although he complained of this. She reported these matters to the doctor, but knowing that paraldehyde is notoriously unpleasant to take he merely advised the continuance of treatment with gargles. Later the same day he returned to see the patient because of continued complaints. When he examined the throat it was red and swollen, with some white patches on it. The following day the patient was seen early in the morning, and the doctor later consulted the hospital pathologist and chief pharmacist to enquire about the possible toxic effects of paraldehyde. He also telephoned the ear nose and throat surgeon, who agreed to see the patient early the following day. Meanwhile penicillin was ordered, but quite suddenly during the afternoon the patient collapsed and, although he recovered for a short time after the administration of oxygen and nikethamide, his condition deteriorated, and he died.

Evidence was given at the inquest by a pathologist that the man had died from acute broncho-pneumonia which had been precipitated by an acute inflammation of the upper respiratory passages, almost certainly caused by the corrosive action of acetic acid which had been present in substantial amount in the paraldehyde solution. He further stated that chemical analysis of the contents of the hospital stock bottle of paraldehyde showed that the substance was old and had undergone serious deterioration by oxidation so that 40 per cent of the contents of the bottle had been converted into acetic acid. Although he found the acid had burned the mouth and air passages, the deceased appeared to have swallowed very little since the stomach was unaffected. He also found that the lungs were extensively infected with both chronic and and more acute tubercular lesions and that, in addition, this disease involved the left kidney. However, while stating that the young man had a serious tubercular infection, he expressed the opinion that the patient would not have died when he did from the disease and he doubted if indeed it was a factor in his death at all.

The verdict at the inquest was death from misadventure, but about nine months later a Writ was issued against the hospital management committee claiming damages on behalf of the deceased's relatives. Since the case was clearly indefensible, solicitors acting for the management committee advised a settlement to which the protection society was invited to contribute. As, however, it was clear that the doctor was in no way to blame, the request was refused and the hospital authority accepted full responsibility.

A general practitioner, on the advice of a consultant gynaecologist, prescribed a valerian and bromide mixture for a patient who had recently had a total hysterectomy. About five months later she developed a rosaceous acne of both cheeks and was referred to a skin specialist, who confirmed the diagnosis and advised appropriate local treatment and phenobarbitone. This treatment was continued for two months, when the skin specialist advised its temporary cessation. Two months after this the patient again attended, requesting further treatment, and the practitioner repeated the prescription for local treatment and also prescribed a vitamin B compound for the acne. Two months later still she asked for a copy of the bromide prescription and implied that his treatment had caused her skin complaint.

The practitioner heard no more of this complaint until seven years later when he found her in his waiting room and she handed him a document which was a High Court Writ. Unfortunately, because it had been completed in the patient's own handwriting, he failed to recognise its significance and paid no attention to it. This was followed by a Statement of Claim received by registered post, but once more, because the document was in the patient's handwriting and looked in no way official, he decided he could safely ignore it. He neither consulted solicitors nor referred the matter to the society, with the result that no defence was entered and the plaintiff accordingly obtained judgment in the sum of £350.

She duly sent bailiffs to the house to levy execution and at this stage the practitioner, greatly distressed, consulted the Society. The society's solicitors were promptly instructed to apply to the court for the judgment to be set aside, and this application was successful. Leave was granted to deliver a defence, provided this was done within fourteen days and the £350 already awarded paid into court pending trial of the action.

When the case finally came to trial the plaintiff maintained that she had earned a living as a model and that before taking the bromide medicine prescribed by the practitioner she had never had any rash affecting her face. Evidence was given by a neighbour that she had previously had a most beautiful complexion and a photograph of her before taking the medicine was put in as evidence. She alleged that within a month she became disfigured, her face being scarlet and covered with yellow pustules and burn-like patches, and that her skin was hot and painful. She also referred to an unpleasant copper taste in her mouth and said that her saliva was blood-stained. In spite of much advice and treatment, the taste and disfigurement had persisted; she was still unable to wash her face, which had to be cleansed with creams and oils, and she was extremely susceptible to heat and light. The only expert testimony submitted on her behalf was two reports from a deceased skin specialist. In the first of these he wrote that he could not contradict her idea that medicine had produced her rash but in the second report he referred to the rosacea as a natural disease.

In giving his judgment his Lordship stated that whereas the plaintiff clearly felt that the whole of her trouble was due to the prescription given to her by her doctor, he was far from satisfied that she had ever suffered from bromide poisoning. He preferred the sworn evidence of the doctors who were called on behalf of the defendant, to the written opinions of a deceased specialist. Furthermore, he felt that even if the plaintiff did suffer from bromide poisoning there was no evidence whatever that the defendant was in any way negligent; on the contrary, there was evidence that he had treated her properly and in accordance with the best standards. Judgment was accordingly given for the doctor with costs and an order made that the sum of £350 which had already been paid into court should be returned.

A patient was admitted to hospital with severe anal pain for which no cause was apparent. A house surgeon, on the instructions of the registrar, injected Proctocaine into the anal sphincter and, as there was a marked tenderness, proposed to insert Xylocaine jelly into the anal canal. A tube of the jelly was requested and brought from the theatre. The member read the name lignocaine on the label but it was found that the jelly could not be expelled from the tube. At this moment the visiting hour began in the ward and the houseman decided to have the patient taken into the theatre where he used a tube of jelly handed to him by an experienced sister, although subsequently he had no certain recollection of asking for Xylocaine or examining the label on the tube. A few hours later a house physician was called to see the patient, who had developed convulsions. No firm diagnosis was made but paraldehyde was given with good effect and when muscle twitchings occurred about two hours later a further dose was administered. Later that evening the house surgeon was called to see the patient and found him dead.

Following an autopsy, analysis showed that the body contained a very large quantity of Nupercaine, which was considered to be the cause of death. Investigations showed that the tube used by the member in the theatre had contained 4 per cent Nupercaine jelly which was made up in the hospital pharmacy and packed in tubes identical with those used for lignocaine. It appeared that the house surgeon had placed the nozzle of the tube in the anal canal and expelled a very indefinite and uncontrolled quantity of the jelly.

Not long after the inquest a claim was lodged. No defence was possible as it was evident that a system which permitted tubes of lignocaine and Nupercaine identical in appearance to be kept together in the theatre was a bad one, and moreover both the sister and house surgeon failed to take the elementary precaution of reading the label. A settlement was therefore negotiated and shared between the hospital authorities and the society.

Surgical

A patient with a history of having fallen on his left elbow was seen in an out-patient department by a surgeon. After X-ray examination it was found that there was no recent bony injury but the tip of the olecranon was separated. Subsequently, the patient was seen on two further occasions and, since he was still complaining of pain, his name was put on the out-patient waiting list for excision of the loose fragment. When his turn came for operation it was unfortunately performed on the wrong elbow which had been prepared in error because of the presence of an enlarged olecranon bursa. Shortly afterwards the surgeon operated on the injured elbow.

Four months later the patient, having been granted a full legal aid certificate, began proceedings against the hospital management committee and the surgeon. In these proceedings the patient alleged that the surgeon was guilty of negligence and/or assault and claimed £73 in respect of loss of earnings. The surgeon had no answer to the claim for assault and in consultation with the solicitors to the hospital management committee the matter was disposed of for a small sum.

A middle-aged lady, who had suffered for some years from chronic sinusitis and recurrent nasal polypi, was admitted to hospital for further operative treatment. A consultant laryngologist performed an intranasal operation involving partial excision of the right middle turbinate bone and removal of polypi adjacent to and arising from the ethmoidal air cells. The operation was uneventful, and before the patient was returned to the ward the surgeon examined her eyes and satisfied himself there was no intra-orbital haemorrhage, but on recovering from the anaesthetic the patient's right eye was swollen, and for two days she was unable to open it. The nursing staff were well aware of this condition but did not regard it as in any way unusual after this type of operation and did not mention the matter to the resident surgical officer who visited the ward daily. Two days after the operation the patient herself remarked that she could not see, but she was assured that her sight would be all right. Four days after the operation the resident surgical officer was asked to see the patient because her eye was still swollen and she continued to complain of lack of vision. On ophthalmoscopy, he saw enough to make him immediately telephone the consultant, who visited the patient and arranged for her immediate transfer to the care of an ophthalmic specialist. The latter found that she had a thrombosis of the central retinal vessels with extensive papilloedema but as the eye had been swollen for four days he decided that a decompression operation would be useless and told the patient that the sight of the right eye had been permanently lost.

Twelve months later solicitors acting for the patient informed the hospital that their client had lost the sight of her eye through the negligence of the surgeon who operated and the nursing staff in whose care she had been. The facts were reported to the society and after obtaining reports from several experts the society's solicitors were instructed to take the necessary steps to defend the surgeon.

When the case came to trial it was alleged against the surgeon that he had caused injury to the right optic nerve and/or bleeding into the orbital tissues of the eye, resulting in damage to the optic nerve and blindness, and that he should have been aware of the possibility of dangerous bleeding and taken the immediate remedial steps required. It was also claimed that he should have warned the nursing staff of the necessity for special vigilance and explained to the patient the inherent danger of the operation.

The expert witness, called to give evidence on behalf of the plaintiff, stated that he himself had had no personal experience of such a complication after this operation and knew of only two cases reported in the literature. He did not think that the occurrence of bleeding behind the eye necessarily indicated lack of skill on the part of the operator but, in a lecture he had given a few months before the date of this operation, he had drawn attention to the possibility that when this type of haemorrhage was recognised early, immediate decompression might prevent permanent damage to the sight.

The surgeon himself testified that he had performed many similar operations, had never experienced such a complication before and, at the time, was unaware of the opinion expressed by the previous witness in his lecture. His operating technique was the same as usual and there was no need to give any special instructions to the nursing staff in this case.

On behalf of the surgeon two experts were called; the ophthalmologist to whom the patient was transferred when the damage to her eye was recognised, and another eminent ophthalmologist. A consultant laryngologist was also in court but Counsel did not find it necessary to ask him to go into the witness box in view of the evidence already given by the plaintiff's own expert which largely supported the defendant's case.

One of the ophthalmological experts produced a skull and gave a lucid exposition of the anatomical relations of the orbit, explaining how retro-orbital haemorrhage could result from operations in the ethmoid region. He said that such a rare accident could not reasonably be anticipated in any particular case and could not be prevented by any known means. He was quite definite that he himself would not advise or undertake decompression in this kind of case as he firmly believed such intervention would almost inevitably do more harm than good.

Judgment was given for the defendants.

A married woman, aged 41, was admitted to hospital for surgical treatment of varicose veins in both legs.

Under an epidural analgesic a consultant surgeon performed a Trendelenberg operation on the right side, extirpating the saphenous trunk from the groin to below the knee with a vein stripper. He then asked his house surgeon, who had assisted him at this and several previous similar operations, if he felt competent to operate on the left leg. The house surgeon agreed and declined the consultant's offer to assist him. The latter accordingly disrobed and shortly afterwards left the theatre to write up his notes in an adjoining staff room.

The next day he learned that there was anxiety about the patient's left foot because it was cold and numb. On examination he confirmed that the foot was cold and 'marbled' in appearance and, being unable to detect any arterial pulsation in the limb, he suspected the possibility of damage to the femoral artery and arranged to explore the operation wound immediately. He found that the common femoral, superficial femoral, and profunda femoris arteries had been ligated and some intervening tissue removed. By extending the wound proximally and distally he mobilised the stump of the common femoral artery and successfully anastomosed it to the upper end of the superficial femoral. When pulsation could be felt in this vessel he injected into it some heparin and, after closing the wound, applied a plaster slab behind the leg and thigh in order to keep the knee flexed and thus minimise tension at the site of the anastomosis. Despite energetic medical treatment, the leg became gangrenous and, four weeks after the original operation, had to be amputated above the knee. The patient made slow and ultimately satisfactory progress, but was not ready for the fitting of an artificial leg until several months had elapsed. In due course the hospital authorities received a letter from solicitors on behalf of the patient making a claim against the hospital and the consultant for the loss of the leg and the pain and suffering caused by the error in the operation.

When the case was considered by the protection society it was clear that no responsibility for what had happened could rest on the hospital except in so far as they were vicariously liable. Although he was not actually present when the error was made by the house surgeon, it was felt that the consultant had some responsibility because he had permitted a relatively inexperienced junior to perform an operation without direct supervision.

After a meeting between representatives of the protection society and the defence union of which the house surgeon was a member, it was agreed that each society should contribute equally to a settlement.

A 36-year-old unmarried labourer, who had twice before had bilateral inguinal herniorraphy performed, suffered recurrence on the left side. Examination by the registrar showed that while the right testicle was normal, the left appeared to be atrophied. These findings were, after admission, confirmed by the consultant, and by the senior registrar, the former explaining to the patient that in order to reduce the possibility of further recurrence of the hernia it would probably be necessary to remove the already useless left testicle.

At operation, carried out by the senior registrar, some difficulty was encountered due to the fibrous tissue resulting from the previous operations, and it was decided that a section of the spermatic cord would have to be excised. On lifting the testis from the scrotum it was found to be much larger than had been anticipated and it appeared to be healthy. The senior registrar therefore sought the opinion of the consultant, who was in the adjoining theatre. He was surprised at the findings, but noted that the cord had necessarily been rather mutilated during the difficult dissection and considered therefore that the blood supply of the testis was of doubtful adequacy. The repair would, he felt, be jeopardised were it to be retained and he therefore concluded that it should be sacrificed. The senior registrar, being so instructed, excised it and concluded the operation.

Postoperatively it was found that the patient's only testicle had been removed. The scrotum and both inguinal regions were somewhat distorted as a result of the previous operations and in fact the true position had been that the only testicle belonged to the left side, the other swelling being a mass connected with the hernial sac. Both consultant and senior registrar stated that it had not occurred to them to doubt the pre-operative findings, or to make any further examination when an apparently normal testicle was exposed during the operation. Further examination of the scrotum at that time would indeed have imperilled asepsis, and while this might have been considered a contra-indication, in all probability it would not have weighed heavily against the danger of castrating the patient, had the possibility that the pre-operative assessment could have been in error been considered.

There were, it should be stressed, no notes of the previous operations to assist in this connection and it was never determined whether the right testicle had been removed surgically or had undergone atrophy.

In due course a claim was made alleging negligence and there being no reasonable prospect of a successful defence, a settlement was finally agreed for a very substantial sum.

A middle-aged woman was admitted to hospital for treatment of an oesophageal stricture caused by her having accidentally taken caustic soda eighteen months previously. The intention was to resect the affected portion of oesophagus and replace it with a graft to be taken from the colon. The patient's blood was grouped and a blood group determination form sent to the ward. The method of inserting pathological reports in patient's files was for them to be stuck on a card from below upwards each report overlapping the previous one. The patient's name appeared on the top of the card but would be obscured when one turned back later reports to look at previous ones. While the insertion of reports was normally the duty of the registered nurse, it appeared in this case that it must have been undertaken by some unqualified person, though her identity was never established. All went well at operation until the chest was opened, when the carotid pulse became impalpable and three pints of blood were sent for. When the particulars on the bottles had been checked against the blood group determination form in the patient's case sheet, the blood was administered. Later in the operation the patient's condition worsened and a further three pints were given after a similar check. By the end of the operation the patient's condition was fair and she recovered consciousness before her return to the ward, but in view of the possibility of oozing from cut surfaces a seventh pint of blood was put up, and two hours after the operation more was ordered from the laboratory. On this occasion the patient's name was taken not from the blood group determination form but from the front of the patient's notes, though the blood group itself and the reference number were taken from the form. It was then discovered that the name did not tally with the blood group and reference number, and enquiries were made. It was found that there were two patients of the same surname but quite different Christian names in the ward, both under the same house surgeon who had been responsible for ordering the blood on the first occasion. These two patients had been admitted and their blood grouped at about the same time, but it was found that the determination forms had been transposed. The house surgeon immediately informed the surgeons concerned and a replacement transfusion of some six pints was carried out, but after an initial improvement the patient's condition deteriorated and she died some nine hours after the end of the operation.

Several months later a claim was made on behalf of the deceased's husband, and the society took the view that the prime responsibility rested on the hospital authorities in respect of the nurse who placed the incorrect blood group determination form in the patient's folder. At the same time it had to be admitted that the house surgeon, in ordering the blood, had a duty to check the patient's name and number on the form with those on the card upon which the forms were stuck or upon the front of the patient's notes. The fact that he had admitted two patients with the same surname to the same ward should, it was felt, have made him particularly careful in this respect. The hospital authority suggested that as they issued a pamphlet regarding the duties of resident medical officers and this laid it down that they were to see that full clinical notes were recorded and all special reports attached thereto, the responsibility was entirely that of the house surgeon. The protection society was not prepared to accept that the hospital authority could evade responsibility in this manner and eventually a very reasonable settlement was reached to which the society contributed one-third.

A five-year-old girl was operated on by an ophthalmic surgeon for her internal strabismus. No abnormality was noted when the surgeon paid his next visit to the hospital five days later, but the following evening the ward sister noticed some swelling of the eyelid. The surgeon saw the child the next day, that is one week after the operation, and found chemosis together with cloudiness of the anterior chamber. He immediately instituted treatment, but as the infecting organism was later identified as a penicillin resistant staphylococcus, this proved unavailing. The child was discharged seven weeks after the operation and followed up in out-patients; when the eye was noted to be shrinking the mother was advised that the question of enucleation be postponed for the time being. She, however, took her daughter to another hospital, where the eye was excised. Some months after this a solicitor's letter was received alleging negligence against the surgeon and the regional hospital board. Matters proceeded slowly and some two years after the operation a Writ was issued.

It appeared that the parent on behalf of the infant was basing her case on pathological reports describing a penetration of the sclera, choroid, and retina, which it was alleged had occurred during the course of the operation.

The protection society, having taken expert opinion, denied liability, and eventually more than five years after the incident the case came before the court. An expert witness, called by the society to support the surgeon, established the fact that the time interval between operation and the first evidence of infection was much greater than would be expected had the infection been introduced in the theatre. The pathologist appearing for the plaintiff admitted in cross-examination that the penetration of the sclera he had described would be more likely to have resulted from infection than from an instrument used during the course of the operation. The judge paid tribute to the skill and care shown by the surgeon and concluded that no case of negligence against him had been made out and the regional hospital board was also exonerated. The plaintiff being legally aided, it was not possible to recover any of the heavy costs incurred in defending against an allegation which arose simply because the patient suffered what the judge described as 'a bit of bad luck'.

A consultant obstetrician performed a lower segment Caesarean section on a private patient suffering from pre-eclamptic toxaemia. The operation proceeded normally until the child was delivered and the umbilical cord cut. At this stage the obstetrician, as was his invariable habit, held the child inverted, with one hand grasping the ankles and the other supporting the neck. It was then the duty of the sister to clamp and cut the cord while the other assistant, in this case the registrar, concentrated on securing haemostasis of the blood sinuses of the lower segment. The sister was seen to clamp the cord twice about 12 inches from the umbilicus, and holding a gauze swab in her left hand, which partly surrounded the cord and prevented the sudden spurt of blood, proceeded to cut the cord with scissors. At that moment something was seen to flutter to the ground; the immediate reaction was that it was part of the gauze swab, but it was quickly found to be the tip of the baby's left ring finger. Immediate steps were taken to re-suture the severed portion and later that day an orthopaedic surgeon trimmed and re-sutured the finger. Fortunately, the nail bed was largely preserved and the deformity was minimal.

Intimation was received from the child's father that he would hold the surgeon responsible for the accident and it was decided that such a claim must be strenuously resisted; this was an accident that should not have happened, but the fact that it did was felt not to be in any way due to the surgeon's lack of care. He was working with an experienced team who had previously assisted him at very many similar operations, and the sister was the senior sister midwife of the maternity unit who had undertaken this comparatively simple procedure countless times and was felt to be an entirely proper person to whom such a procedure might be delegated. It was argued by the father that the surgeon's duty was to exercise such a degree of supervision that such accidents could not happen and that he had failed to do this. At such a moment, however, he could not divide his attention between mother and child, and both hands would be occupied holding the baby. While he could, and no doubt would, exercise overall supervision, it could not be admitted that this must be so close as to guarantee that such accident could ever happen, and it seemed proper that such an action as cutting the cord should be delegated to a trained midwife, as a duty performed by midwives from time immemorial.

The surgeon was reluctant to press for his proper fees in this case, but it was urged upon him that he should do so. This was met by a defence and counterclaim based on the contentions already put forward by the father. The case was heard in due course, when the Judge gave judgment for the surgeon, dismissing the counterclaim and saying that the member was clearly not responsible for this unfortunate accident, having throughout exercised the degree of care and skill that was required.

In 1959, a surgeon repaired a right inguinal hernia after two earlier attempts at operative cure had failed. Because of this unfortunate history the surgeon was especially careful to make a strong repair, and in so doing left the internal ring fairly tight. Haematoma was minimal, the wound healed well, skin sutures were removed on the seventh day, and the patient was discharged a week later.

When the patient was subsequently seen the surgeon found thrombosis of the right spermatic cord and a hard 'high lying' testicle, but the herniorraphy was otherwise satisfactory. Three months after the operation the patient resumed work, but on at least two occasions subsequently reported pain in the right groin. When examined, there was no recurrence of the hernia but the right testicle remained in the upper part of the scrotum. The man continued at work for several months, despite pain in the groin, which had become constant. To relieve this his own doctor decided to remove the testicle, which he considered had become atrophic and the source of the trouble. However, the patient was still dissatisfied, and after a few months the surgeon received a letter from solicitors in which proceedings were threatened unless he admitted liability for the loss of their client's testicle as a result of negligent treatment. The surgeon claimed that to achieve a good result in this kind of case a tight repair was essential, although this, in turn, necessarily involved some risk to the blood supply of the testicle and to its ultimate survival as an effective organ. In this instance he admitted atrophy had supervened, but with an intact left testicle the patient suffered no disability or loss of virility.

When the action was heard, the plaintiff's counsel made no complaint about the hernia operation itself but pleaded that postoperative attention was either lacking or entirely unsatisfactory. In the course of his evidence the plaintiff gave a macabre description of one incident of his postoperative care. He stated that he had been, 'held down forcibly on a bed in a two-bed ward in hospital with four nurses holding his arms and legs (one to each) and a man holding his head while the defendant jabbed something about the size of a pencil into his scrotum, withdrew it and jabbed it in again, then squeezed the scrotum and the blood spurted out all over the doctor's shirt and tie and over the two nurses who were holding his legs and over the bed and up on to the ceiling from whence it dripped down on the other bed in the ward',

The general practitioner gave evidence that he removed the patient's testicle seventeen months after the hernia operation because it had atrophied and was causing pain. Another medical witness called on behalf of the plaintiff said that after his examination he considered the patient's complaint of pain to be genuine but believed it was psychological in origin and not due to any physical cause.

The defendant's evidence and cross-examination occupied nearly two days, and a number of witnesses were called on his behalf, including two surgeons as expert witnesses, one of whom expressed the view that it would be impossible for blood to spurt out of a cannula inserted into a haematoma in the scrotum so as to hit a ceiling.

At the end of the case the Judge held that there was no evidence to support three of the six counts, and after a summing-up favourable to the defendant the jury returned a verdict for him in respect of the remaining counts.

A cystoscopy was being performed on a patient with recurring cystitis. An IVP while not conclusive, had suggested an abnormality of the right kidney, and so an attempt was made to pass a ureteric catheter. This part of the operation was carried out by the assistant RSO, but difficulty was experienced in entering the ureteric orifice. The surgical registrar then took over and was surprised to see what looked like a piece of wire lying in the bladder. This proved impossible to remove per urethram and a cystotomy was necessary to recover the object, which was found to be a shaving from a ureteric catheter. After the operation a similar type of catheter was fitted to the cystoscope but could not be made to strip, and it was assumed that the original ureteric catheter had been faulty. Later, however, it was realised that the experiment had been made with a catheter a size smaller than that used at operation. The experiment was thereupon repeated using the same size, as well as type, of catheter and it was found to strip each time, exactly as it had at operation, on the worn and sharp edge of the cystoscope tube.

The question of liability now arose. Was this accident to be blamed on the operator, because the worn and sharp edge was clearly visible to the naked eye and, it could be argued, should have been seen by the type of inspection a careful surgeon should normally make before using an instrument? On the other hand, should not the surgeon reasonably expect that instruments supplied for his use would be properly maintained and inspected by the theatre staff to discover such defects, and should he not

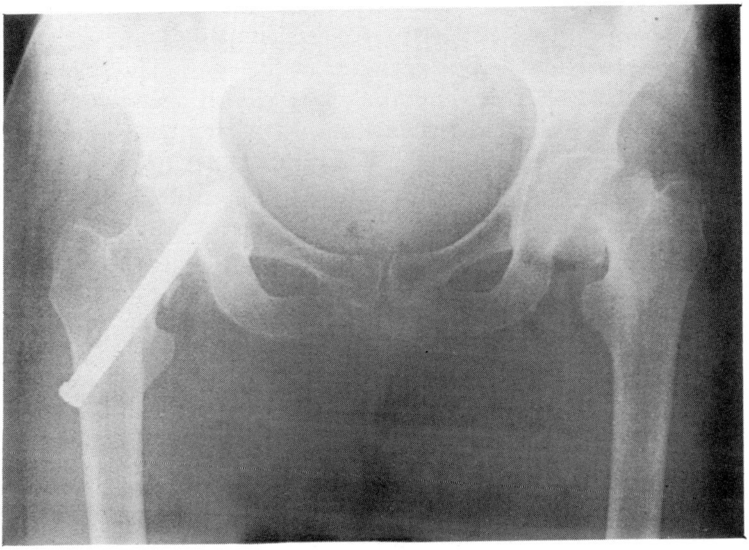

Fig. 20

be entitled to rely on the staff in such matters? Both points of view were put, and forcibly argued with the result that it was agreed that the only fair solution was an equal apportionment. The claim, that had by now arisen, was thus settled for a modest sum on this basis.

Figure 20 is not thought to require any comment.

Miscellaneous

A youth of eighteen attended for a medical examination at a recruiting centre. When the doctor came to examine his ears both were full of wax. He therefore syringed them. There was no difficulty with the right ear but on the left side, although part of the wax came away, there still remained some which was firmly fixed. He therefore decided to soften it by instilling some oil into the ear and told the youth to return after the other members of the board had completed their examination of him. About an hour later further syringing still did not completely clear the ear, which by now was becoming painful. For this reason the doctor let the boy wait again before trying once more. The third and last effort to eliminate the wax proved so painful that the doctor desisted, instilled more oil into the ear and told the young man to return a week later. He also gave him some oil and instructed him how to use it. The boy reported at the examination centre a week later with a piece of lint over his ear on which was some brownish yellow discharge. On enquiry the member found that the boy had had some bleeding from the ear during the evening of the day when it had been syringed, had consulted his doctor and had been seen by a specialist. On examination the ear was found to be clear of debris and there was a small perforation in the tympanum. In a questionnaire completed prior to his examination by the medical board, the boy had stated that he had had no trouble with his ears; he was also asked the same question by the doctor and again answered 'no'. Some time later the boy, through his sister, consulted solicitors who made a claim against the Ministry. It is believed that the Ministry made him an *ex gratia* offer of a small sum, which was declined. Ultimately, the boy, through his sister as next friend, instituted proceedings against the doctor alleging that he had perforated his left tympanum while examining his ear.

The papers were submitted to two experienced otologists, both of whom were of the opinion that it is impossible to perforate a healthy eardrum by syringing. In view of this it was decided that the proceedings should be defended. At the trial at the local Assizes the boy, as was to be expected, declared that prior to his examination at the recruiting centre his hearing was perfect. The expert called on his behalf stated quite frankly in his evidence that perforation could not be caused by ordinary syringing and there must have been previous damage of which the patient knew nothing. In view of this and the evidence of the experts called on behalf of the doctor, the Judge gave judgment for the doctor with costs.

A resident medical officer had under her care a patient suffering from a tuberculous empyema which was to be aspirated twice weekly on the instructions of the consultant physician. On one such occasion she had aspirated both the pus and air when the patient suddenly complained of feeling faint. It was immediately realised that air embolism might have occurred, and the needle was withdrawn. The patient lost consciousness and was obviously shocked. She was laid flat on the couch with the foot raised and almost immediately she became conscious and rational for a short time before relapsing into unconsciousness for about ten minutes.

Later she complained of severe headache, became extremely restless, and developed flaccid and later spastic paralysis of the left arm and left leg, with transient signs of involvement of the ocular muscles. The paralytic symptoms persisted and fourteen months later it was stated that she was still unable to move her left arm, shoulder, hand, leg, and foot. Sensation on the left side was slightly impaired and there was spinal scoliosis in the dorsal region with complaints of recurrent pain in the left upper arm and left hip.

When a claim had been made, experts were consulted and agreed that the paralysis had been caused by air embolism. One expert advanced several theories as to how this could have occurred and stated that the risks of such an accident were inevitable but slight, and that in this case no blame could be attached to the operator. Another suggested that air might have been introduced into the vein through faulty technique. He pointed out that in clearing the blocked needle into the pleural cavity by depressing the plunger of the syringe while the point of the needle was in the pus, 2 or 3 ml of air might have been injected. He considered that this method of clearing a blocked needle during an aspiration was never justifiable, and when this proposition was put to the other expert he found himself forced to agree.

Counsel advised that it would be difficult to defend the claim since the experts concurred that the member's faulty technique could have caused the air embolus, although they agreed that it might have arisen in several other ways. A settlement was therefore negotiated.

Dr A, practising in the Republic of Ireland, had accepted a patient for treatment under the maternity scheme and happened to be out when the patient went into premature labour. The husband therefore called in another doctor (Dr B) who visited the patient and dealt with a retained placenta. Dr A was informed and saw the patient the following day, and in view of her poor condition sent her to hospital where further placental fragments were removed.

Dr B subsequently rendered to the patient's husband an account for 25 guineas for his one attendance on the patient. The husband declined to pay on the grounds that the fee was excessive. In order to assist the husband in meeting the expense to which he had been put through having to call another doctor for the confinement, Dr A paid over to the husband the fee of £7 7s. 0d., which he was entitled to claim from the local authority under the maternity scheme. The husband added £2 2s. 0d. and offered Dr B £9 9s. 0d. in settlement of his account, which Dr B refused to accept. Dr B then sued the husband for the full amount and obtained judgment.

The patient and her husband thereupon began proceedings against the local authority and against Dr A, alleging that the former had been in breach of a statutory duty to make available to the wife midwifery services pursuant to the Health Act, 1953, and that Dr A, having accepted the wife as a patient under the maternity scheme, was in breach of contract through having failed to attend at the confinement. In the result the husband had been ordered to pay Dr B's fee and legal costs, as well as his own costs in resisting the claim, and the action against the local authority and Dr A was brought with a view to recovering these items as damages.

Delivering judgment, the Judge held that the local authority had discharged its duty under the statute and he dismissed the claim against them. Dealing with the claim against Dr A, the Judge said that his failure to be available on the night that the patient went unexpectedly into labour was not a breach of any duty he owed her and was not negligence on his part. He said that the allegation that the member was negligent in not being available or in failing to provide a deputy was not acceptable as it required a doctor to do the impossible. 'One of the more glaring anomalies', he stated, 'flowing from these propositions is that the doctor could never treat any patient save in his own consulting room for fear that, should he go out to a patient, another patient needing attention at his home would then have a cause of complaint and the doctor's dilemma would then be complete and unique, for he is bound by the agreement to attend his patients at their homes if necessary'.

The action against the doctor was dismissed and a notice of appeal served by the plaintiffs was subsequently withdrawn.

A general practitioner attended a patient who suffered among other things from osteo-arthritis, deafness, and hypertrophy of the prostate, so that he had for many years been under the care of consultants and his own doctor.

Following a prostatectomy, the patient was discharged from hospital, was visited two or three times a week at home and, eventually, two and a half months after the operation, the final certificate was given. Physiotherapy had been arranged at a local hospital during this period in respect of the osteo-arthritis.

About a year after the patient returned to work and while still on the doctor's list he instituted proceedings against the doctor, alleging neglect in that he had been certified as fit for work too early; had not been referred to the hospital of his choice for physiotherapy; that the certificate had not stipulated that he was fit for only light work; and that general neglect had deprived him of the benefits of the national health service. Damages of £400 were claimed.

The Judge found that, far from neglect, the doctor had given every attention and the claim was dismissed with costs, but as the plaintiff was living on national assistance and supported by legal aid there was clearly no hope of recovering any of these costs, which were substantial. Shortly afterwards the patient wrote to the protection society's solicitors stating his intention of lodging an appeal. The plaintiff's subsequent application for leave to appeal out of time was dismissed.

At 10.0 p.m. on 30th December 1956 in an Australian holiday resort, a train of events started which led to a young woman's death and culminated, five years later, in a legal action against two doctors.

The history of the case was that as this girl was walking along a path at a mountain health resort, she felt a 'sting' on the left foot. No reptile or insect was seen, but an eye witness subsequently stated that she thought she saw a 'round bodied thing like a rat' scuttle off into the nearby bush. Almost at once the wound was examined by her friends and the hotel proprietor and as there were no apparent punctures but rather scratches, the suggestion of a snake-bite was rejected in favour of an insect sting. There was much local pain, and the foot soon swelled up with an area of discoloration around the wound like a bruise. Within five minutes she vomited and later had severe colic and diarrhoea; friends described her as being in a state of nervous collapse. As she was obviously very ill, an ambulance was summoned and she was taken to the nearest hospital, about thirty miles away, where she was seen at 2.30 a.m. by Dr A who had been warned at midnight by the local ambulance superintendent that he had been asked to bring in a patient who was suffering from 'query snake-bite' sustained earlier that night. When he saw the girl she was very nervous and agitated, complained of pain in the foot and told him of the vomiting; on examination he found an abrasion about one eighth of an inch long on the dorsum of the foot near the base of the little toe. He did not think it resembled a snake-bite but as she had been wearing sandals he thought the scratch could have been caused by one fang, the sandal strap arresting the other. If indeed the injury had been caused by a snake, he did not think the linear scratch would have allowed any poison to enter the blood stream. Examination of the nervous system did not show any signs of snake-venom poisoning and as four hours had elapsed since the incident he did not consider the patient to be in danger. Dr A saw the patient again about ten hours later when he found her general condition satisfactory apart from a complaint of a sore throat which he found mildly inflamed; her swallowing reflexes were normal. He ordered daily doses of penicillin and considered nothing more was required.

The next day he was off duty so his partner, Dr B, saw the patient at the request of the hospital matron who telephoned at 6.0 a.m. to report that the girl was complaining of difficulty with her breathing. He made a thorough examination of the patient's chest and nervous system but was satisfied there were no signs of snake-bite poisoning and that the wound did not suggest such a diagnosis. On questioning a friend he learnt that the patient had been previously treated for a neurotic condition and there was a family history of neurosis, but he was not inclined to dismiss her symptoms as functional in origin until she had been under observation a little longer. The question of her return home was then raised, and Dr B gave his consent to her discharge provided she was taken direct to hospital, to which she was admitted at 12.30

p.m. She was there found to be gravely ill but gave a lucid history, saying that she had noticed the onset of general weakness the previous evening and that this had steadily increased. She had tried to walk to the car in which she was brought to the hospital but was unable to stand. She had also had difficulty in swallowing and breathing and these symptoms were increasing in severity. On examination there was muscular weakness, she could not swallow or protrude her tongue, and paralysis of diaphragm and accessory muscles of respiration was almost complete. There was no loss of sensation, but some stiffness of back and neck. In respect of the injury the consultant at the hospital stated, 'on the left foot there were several minute puncture wounds and one slightly larger puncture wound, but the appearance was not typical of snake-bite. There was some discoloration of the skin around the wound'.

Lumbar puncture was performed and, pending laboratory examination, a diagnosis of poliomyelitis was seriously considered but the spinal fluid was found to be normal whereas in her urine there was evidence of kidney damage and haemolysis. With these findings, the gross neurological phenomena and the history, a diagnosis of snake-bite was considered reasonably certain. The reptile responsible was thought most likely to have been Tropidechis carinatus; this snake was known to be not uncommon in the district concerned, was nocturnal in its habits, pugnacious, and had strongly neurotoxic venom. Despite treatment in an iron lung and large doses of anti-venene the respiratory paralysis and other symptoms did not respond and chest complications preceded her death on 9th January. After an autopsy, death was reported to be due to acute pulmonary oedema complicating bulbar and respiratory paralysis. An inquest was opened by the city coroner in July 1957 and was finally closed on 2nd May the next year. Evidence from all relevant sources was given in great detail and both doctors attended as witnesses but without legal representation. The coroner finally attributed the girl's death from snake-bite 'to undue delay in combating the venom' and a 'fatal error' in the original medical treatment and diagnosis.

A claim followed and the trial took place in December 1961. After a hearing lasting four days the jury found that the two doctors had not been negligent and judgment was entered for the defendants with costs.

On 12th November 1957, twenty-four hours before a liner was due to sail from Sydney to Auckland, one of her crew fell in the engine room and injured his right knee. This man of fifty-eight was seen immediately after the incident by the assistant ship-surgeon who found the knee tender and swollen but freely movable. He was sent to rest in his bunk and the next morning was examined by the senior surgeon. This doctor confirmed the findings of his colleague but noted limitation of movement and the presence of an old surgical incision over the medial aspect of the joint. X-ray examination showed a recent intercondylar fracture of the lower end of the femur with separation of the medial condyle and involvement of the articular surface. By this time the ship was about to leave port or had already done so and in the circumstances he considered it was reasonable to treat the patient on board; the leg was therefore put up in a Thomas splint. When three days later the ship docked at Auckland the surgeon told the injured man that he would have to be landed there and transferred to hospital. However, with 'an old sailor's dread of being left in a strange port', he implored the doctor to let him remain on the ship and continue with his treatment. His entreaties, unfortunately as it turned out, were successful as with some reluctance the doctor gave way. The leg was then placed in a Braun splint and after the swelling had subsided the medial condyle was manipulated into a satisfactory position under general anaesthesia and the limb encased in a full-length plaster, which was not removed until thirty-five days later. From the end of December 1957, until the ship docked at Tilbury in February 1958, the man was able to undertake light duties but was referred to hospital for physiotherapy. A few months later the injured knee became increasingly painful and an orthopaedic surgeon advised an arthrodesis which was performed in August 1958. Shortly after, arthritic symptoms developed in the left knee but surgical removal of the patella was apparently very successful. About this time the seaman's union first approached the shipping company on behalf of their member and raised the question of a claim. The statement of claim made it clear that the plaintiff's only allegations were of medical negligence. Up-to-date reports were now obtained from experts and the papers referred to Counsel for an opinion. He pointed out that all the experts were agreed that this kind of fracture should (whenever practicable) be dealt with by open operation since only by this means can satisfactory reduction be maintained. It followed that if the ship was still in port when the fracture was first diagnosed as such it would have been better to put the patient ashore and admit him to hospital. Even three days later when the ship reached Auckland it would still have been wiser to do this for, although the doctor's reluctant decision to keep his patient on the ship was on humanitarian grounds understandable, if any misfortune resulted the doctor concerned must accept responsibilty. Counsel therefore considered that the plaintiff was likely to succeed upon the issue of liability, but thought something could be made of the issue of causation. In support he referred to one expert's opinion that 'the pre-existing osteoarthritic condition of the plaintiff's right knee meant that surgical treatment was not bound to produce a significantly better result than conservative treatment' and that 'an arthrodesis after a fracture of this kind would have been necessary anyhow' He estimated the value of the claim at £1,000-£1,250 and in the light of his opinions it was decided that a settlement for anything less than £1,000 would be advantageous. When, very soon after this decision had been reached, it was confirmed by reference to the ship's log that the liner was still in Sydney harbour when the diagnosis was established in the first place, settlement for a sum substantially less than £1,000 was negotiated.

On 22nd February 1963 a young woman aged nineteen years submitted to treatment for a severe idiopathic scoliosis of her lower thoracic spine. An orthopaedic surgeon fitted her with a 'full body plaster' in which he incorporated a metal frame. Three days later the report of an X-ray examination was satisfactory and during the next ten days the plaster was bivalved and turnbuckles fitted to the metal frame. On 27th March X-ray examination showed some slight reduction in the deformity but also revealed the presence of a hairpin in or under the plaster. The significance of this finding was not appreciated at the time, and when another X-ray film was taken on 17th April the pin was seen still to be present, a fact pointed out by the radiologist. About this time the patient's general condition began to decline and she was complaining of backache and lack of appetite. On 25th April, after some discharge was observed to be coming from underneath the plaster, a window was cut out under the lower part of the right scapula. This disclosed an area of infection 3 inches in diameter and a central slough in which a hairpin was found embedded. Over the next five days the patient developed difficulty in breathing and pain in the upper abdomen. By 1st May the patient's symptoms of trismus and flexor spasms in her limbs established the diagnosis of tetanus and rendered the removal of the plaster essential. There followed a period of nine days when the patient was gravely ill, but after 9th May she rapidly improved and was able to leave the hospital at the end of the month. Unfortunately, owing to the necessary premature removal of the plaster all improvement in the patient's scoliosis was lost and she had to face once again the ordeal of a long period of uncomfortable immobilisation.

During her stay in hospital culminating in a terrifying illness which was nearly fatal, the patient, a shy young woman, displayed a high degree of courage and fortitude, but her mother's attitude became increasingly hostile and aggressive. It was not therefore surprising that her complaint to the Ministry of Health about the treatment of her daughter at the hospital was soon followed by a civil claim alleging negligence against the hospital and its staff.

Initially, expert opinion was favourable, liability was denied, and a successful defence seemed possible. Later, however, it became clear that the expert witnesses would be likely to concede under cross-examination that the X-ray findings of 27th March, and even more so those of 17th April, should have been followed by further investigation. It seemed probable that if a window had been cut in the back of the plaster at that time the hairpin could have been removed before the development of closed sepsis which subsequently provided such ideal conditions for the growth of tetanus organisms. Another point that had originally seemed of minor importance was that the patient after admission to hospital had been allowed to retain her long and abundant hair which necessitated the use of numerous hairpins. When later she was treated in a different hospital, the surgeon had insisted that her long hair must be sacrificed, presumably on the grounds that hairpins have a notorious tendency to find their way under plaster casts.

Faced then with a plaintiff whose long stay in hospital had been all to no purpose and who, moreover, had nearly died from a painful complication it was essential to present to the jury unassailable medical testimony in support of the defendant's clinical judgment and actions. Evidence of this strength was not forthcoming and a negotiated settlement was considered necessary; this was ultimately achieved with a small contribution from the hospital's insurers.

A twenty-seven-year old woman was admitted for rest and observation to the antenatal ward in the thirty-second week of a twin pregnancy. She had early signs of pre-eclamptic toxaemia and her previous delivery had been by Caesarian section. She remained in the hospital until full-term, at which stage it was decided that labour should be induced. The house officer was instructed to set up a Syntocinon drip. He set the infusion at 7.0 p.m. using a half litre bottle of 5 per cent glucose as diluent. Twenty minutes later he was informed over the telephone that the patient was having a rigor. He thereupon ordered the drip to be stopped. One hour later, when a further call from the ward informed the house officer that the patient's temperature had shot up to 104° F, he went to the ward immediately and was joined by the registrar. The patient was in advanced labour and healthy male twins were delivered normally shortly afterwards. The patient's condition had become extremely critical, acute circulatory collapse supervened, and she died 3½ hours after the start of the Syntocinon drip.

Post-mortem examination revealed the cause of death as septicaemia due to intravenous infusion of contaminated fluid. The remainder of the contents of the glucose bottle had been examined by the bacteriologist 15 hours after the patient's death. The fluid was seen to be opalescent in a good light and on culture grew bacteria of the aeromonas group identical to those cultured from the patient's blood.

Subsequently a writ was issued against the hospital and later the house officer and manufacturers of the infusion were joined as defendants. The protection society firmly held the view that no liability could rest with the house officer who had set up the drip. This had been done in the evening not under optimal lighting conditions and in such circumstances it was felt he was entitled to rely on the purity of the solution dispensed by the hospital pharmacy.

The hospital board took the view that a substantial contribution to the damages should be made both by the manufacturers and the protection society. The society could not accept this viewpoint and were prepared to defend the action in court. This, however, did not prove to be necessary as finally the manufacturers accepted full liability.

5. Negligence in Communication

As more and more doctors and paramedical workers become involved in a patient's treatment, so more and more can misunderstandings arise between them which, should the patient suffer damage thereby, the law might hold to amount to negligence. The danger of verbal instructions to a patient is only too apparent – *vide supra Coles* v. *Reading H.M.C.* on page 26. Errors in the general practitioner's letter of referral, e.g. left for right, can so easily be copied on to the patient's notes, illegible handwriting, confusion as to the writer of any particular entry, failure to see X-ray or pathological reports which have become buried in the voluminous folder, drug sensitivity either unrecorded or unobserved, all add their tally. When the computer takes over and on-line visual display terminals are available to accompany the doctor on his round, fresh problems will undoubtedly arise, not least of which will be the acceptability of such records in a court of law. Problems of communication should, however, be greatly reduced but until that day comes perhaps the following cases will stress the need for unending vigilance.

A patient attended her doctor's surgery, having just recovered from a bout of influenza which at that time was rife in the district. She said her husband had a headache and backache and the doctor prescribed tablets for these complaints but no request was made for a visit. The next day she returned saying the tablets made her husband sweat, and requested a visit, but unfortunately she did not tell the doctor that they had recently changed their address. Accordingly he made his call to the only address known to him, namely that on the relevant NHS record card. He called more than once but got no response when he rang the doorbell. On looking through a window he saw the place was empty and realised that they must have left and gone elsewhere without informing him.

Before leaving he rang the bell of an adjoining flat to make appropriate inquiries but got no reply. Having other urgent visits to do he continued his rounds, fully expecting to hear from the patient's wife if her husband's condition became worse.

He heard nothing further that day nor the next but the following day, forty-eight hours after the original request for a visit, she came to the surgery and, reporting that her husband was very bad, requested a visit, and gave for the first time their new address. On calling, the doctor found the patient to be suffering from bronchitis, and to be seriously ill, and arranged for his immediate admission to hospital, where he died two days later despite the best of medical attention.

Shortly afterwards the doctor received a solicitor's letter alleging that he had been negligent in failing to visit the patient when first requested to do so and claiming damages on behalf of the widow. Liability was promptly denied and nothing was heard of the matter until a writ and statement of claim were received two years later. After another interval of two years, the case came to trial. The plaintiff's case was that the doctor had been remiss in prescribing codeine before seeing the patient when first asked to do so, and in doing nothing further until forty-eight hours had elapsed, when it was too late. She claimed that earlier attention would have saved her husband's life, but the consultant from the hospital where the patient was treated gave evidence as to the severity of the influenza epidemic and its likely effect upon an elderly chronic bronchitic. He was unable to agree that earlier treatment would have almost certainly made a difference to the outcome.

In his summing up the Judge referred to 'two vital issues of fact.' Was it true that the doctor had attempted to visit the patient on the first occasion he was requested to do so? Was it true that up to that time he had not been informed of the change of address? His Lordship said that the plaintiff in evidence had bitterly criticised the doctor and in speaking of events happening years earlier 'she was obviously incapable of taking a detached fair view' so that 'it would be dangerous to rely upon her recollection'. The doctor, however, impressed the Judge much more favourably and he accordingly accepted his version of what happened. He thought there was some force in the contention that he might have done more when he found his patient had moved but in all the circumstances he did not find this failure to amount to negligence.

A general practitioner was awakened by a telephone call one night at about 11.30. The caller requested a visit for her husband who, she said, was complaining of abdominal pain, and vomiting. The doctor informed her that his partner was on duty and advised that he be contacted. The caller replied that she had tried to ring the partner but had been unable to obtain any reply and it was agreed that she would make another attempt and ring back if necessary. A few minutes later she rang back to say that there was still no reply, and the doctor, thinking that his partner might be visiting a medical neighbour, said he would try to contact him there. This he did, only to be told that his partner had, in fact, called earlier in the evening but had returned home some hours before. He therefore rang his partner's number and heard the engaged tone which was still ringing when he tried again after a short pause. Assuming that the caller must now be speaking to his partner he returned to bed. In point of fact the caller had, following the second conversation, assumed that one or other doctor would attend and returned to her home to await his arrival. The doctor heard nothing more of the matter till he met his partner the following day. The partner had received a telephone call at about 4.30 a.m. and had been told that the caller had made repeated unsuccessful attempts to contact him earlier. As he had been at home since 9 p.m. he assumed that his telephone must be out of order. The patient, whom he knew well, had had an abdominal wound during the war which had necessitated a splenectomy and he had for some years been subject to bouts of vomiting lasting for some hours, which had been investigated without any abnormality being discovered. It had been believed that adhesions, or a diaphragmatic hernia were responsible for the symptoms and that there was no indication for surgery. On this occasion the doctor considered that it was another such attack and advised that a household remedy which had seemed to be efficacious in the past be given, asking also that he be informed if all was not well in an hour's time. At about 6 a.m. he was again called and told that the patient was in agony. He immediately visited, diagnosed an acute abdomen, and referred the patient to hospital where he was admitted at about 8 a.m.

The provisionally registered house surgeon who saw the patient made a tentative diagnosis of small bowel obstruction or, alternatively, cardiac infarction. She ordered chest and abdominal X-rays and an ECG, and while the latter was being taken the patient collapsed and died one and a half to two hours after his arrival in the hospital. Post-mortem examination showed that 16 inches of small bowel and 3 inches of the transverse colon had passed through the diaphragm, resulting in complete intestinal obstruction, and the ECG tracing showed evidence of anterior infarction.

A complaint to the Executive Council was followed by a medical service committee hearing and both practitioners were found in breach of their terms of service, fines of £50 each being recommended. The doctors appealed and their appeals were dismissed by the Minister, the penalties being increased.

Claims for damages were then lodged against both partners, alleging negligence and breach of contract. It was at this point that the society first heard of the matter. A writ was issued citing both general practitioners, the hospital management committee and the house surgeon.

In considering what action to take it was appreciated that the practitioner had believed that his partner would attend the patient but it was not thought that a court would accept that this assumption was in all the circumstances reasonable. It was considered that a court must decide that he should have taken further steps to assure himself that the patient was receiving attention, and that therefore the case was indefensible. Another society, representing the partner, came to a like conclusion, and it was agreed that no liability fell on the hospital or the house surgeon. The claim was therefore settled for a substantial sum, to which each society contributed equally.

A patient attended a casualty department after having fallen through a skylight. In examining an X-ray of her ankle the doctor on casualty duty did not detect any bony injury on the wet film. The radiologist's report, delivered the following day, drew attention to a fracture of the medial malleolus but this report was duly filed away, there being no system for ensuring that it was brought to the notice of any clinician. During the ensuing months the patient saw no fewer than four doctors because of trouble with her ankle and no doubt the history they obtained of her having had an X-ray satisfied them that they were dealing with a soft tissue injury. Eventually, a further X-ray was taken at another hospital and the fracture came to light.

A claim was lodged alleging negligence and on the above facts it was clear that there could be no defence. The liability was, of course, limited to the loss and damage resulting from the delay in diagnosis and the hospital authority agreed to accept 50 per cent of this in view of its failure to institute a system that ensured that radiologist's reports were brought to the notice of the appropriate clinician.

A married woman of twenty-four, with a long and unfortunate psychiatric history of childhood stealing and, later, attempts at suicide, apparently sought to repeat this by jumping out of an upper window of her house. All she in fact achieved was injury to her leg and she was taken to hospital for examination and treatment. Here she was seen by a junior hospital medical officer in the casualty department. He examined her carefully and diagnosed a fracture of the lower end of the right fibula with query fracture of the os calcis. He immobilised the leg in a plaster slab, prescribed an analgesic, and arranged for her to return next morning when X-ray facilities were available. Radiographs were taken at this attendance and when the casualty officer examined them in their wet state he did not find any bone injury. As the patient was already immobilised in a back slab he advised no weight-bearing on crutches for ten days, with the foot elevated as much as possible, and referred her back to her own doctor. In the course of time the dry films were reported upon, the diagnosis being 'fractured os calcis. Position satisfactory',

Because of continuing discomfort, however, her doctor referred her back to the hospital, where the fracture was reviewed again. It was thought that in view of the very slight displacement no further treatment would probably be necessary, but as the foot was reported to be still giving trouble, manipulation was attempted. This resulted in only temporary improvement and eventually a triple arthrodesis was performed.

Some time later a claim was received against the hospital alleging negligence on the grounds of the delay in diagnosis of the fracture which, it was said, aggravated the injury and led to the eventual operation of arthrodesis. Two points seemed to arise; first, whether there had in fact been any negligence on the part of those treating her, and second, whether she had suffered as a result. As regards the first, it could not be denied that there was a lack of liaison between the X-ray department and the casualty officer in the matter of X-ray reports. The practice seemed to be that all these were sent to the casualty department where the sister in charge compared them with the notes, and if there was any discrepancy, such as a fracture that had not been diagnosed, this was brought to the notice of the doctor. In this case the sister thought that she remembered noticing the discrepancy and drawing the casualty officer's attention to it, whereas he was equally certain that this was not so. As two years had passed since the incident it did not seem that anything useful could be achieved by trying to tax memories further, and it was agreed that in the circumstances any settlement should properly be on a 50-50 basis between the protection society and the hospital. As regards the patient's actual loss it was strongly argued that the probable consequences of the type of fracture she had sustained would have been the same whether or not diagnosis had been made at the first attendance, and that any damages must therefore be small. It was a fact that although a fracture was present, there was the minimum of displacement, and one orthopaedic expert went so far as to say that he believed the most effective treatment for such cases was what he referred to as 'supervised neglect', by which he meant a policy of early mobility after a short period of immobilisation. After considerable negotiation settlement was effected for a small sum shared equally between the protection society and the hospital authority.

A house surgeon on casualty duty one night saw a fifteen-year-old boy who had been involved in a fight and was complaining, *inter alia,* of a bruised jaw. A radiographer was summoned and the house surgeon, unable to detect any evidence of bony injury on the wet films, applied a barrel bandage and sent the boy home with an appointment to return six days later when the X-ray report would, it was anticipated, be available. The patient duly attended, had little in the way of symptoms or signs, but the casualty registrar who saw him was unable to find the X-ray report and therefore gave him a further appointment. Later the same day the casualty registrar was handed the X-ray report which referred to an oblique fracture in the symphysis region and a vertical fracture of the right ascending ramus without displacement. The registrar immediately arranged to have the patient recalled.

Two days later the boy was admitted, reduction and internal fixation were carried out, with good results. An allegation of negligence soon followed, which the solicitors representing the hospital authority stated could only be medical in that it related to the failure of the house surgeon and the casualty registrar to make the correct diagnosis. The claim was grossly exaggerated and in parts downright untrue, for it was said that the jaw had had to be refractured and that the delay had made the operation less successful than would otherwise have been the case. In point of fact the consultant who had handled the case and who had consulted the protection society regarding his report stated that the delay had not affected the prognosis.

The society acting for the house surgeon took the view that his examination of the wet plates had been adequate and that the only unsatisfactory feature of the case was the undue delay in the X-ray report reaching the casualty department, a delay which was considered to be entirely unacceptable. Liability was therefore denied on the house surgeon's behalf and in due course it was heard that the hospital authority had settled the claim for very much less than the sum originally demanded.

A girl of twenty years, with a lump in the left breast, was seen in a hospital out-patient department by a consultant surgeon. The lump was noted on the case-sheets, together with a rough drawing indicating its position below the left nipple. In the course of time the patient was admitted for removal of the lump and, at admission, the note was made again that the site was 'under the nipple', At operation next day the registrar, who had not seen the patient before her admission, excised a lump from the upper and outer quadrant of the left breast. This he described as a firm, nodular mass of greyish white tissue measuring 2 cm in diameter. Subsequent microscopy showed benign fibroadenosis. The patient returned home on the fifth day, to return later as an out-patient. Here she once more saw the surgeon who had first seen her and he realised that the original lump was still present. She was therefore again put down for admission for excision of this tumour.

In due course a claim followed demanding damages for what she was alleged to have suffered. It seemed that any fault that there may have been was entirely that of the registrar who had operated, and that this case should be settled. The amount claimed by the patient was, in the event, ridiculously high but the claim was eventually settled at less than a quarter of this figure.

In the early hours of the morning a four-year-old child was brought to hospital by his parents with a history of abdominal pain and vomiting. The general practitioner had diagnosed acute appendicitis with possible perforation but both the house surgeon and surgical registrar found no definite signs of this condition and thought that constipation was the probable cause of the trouble. The parents were upset that, because no private bed was available, the child had been admitted to the general ward which they thought was understaffed. They returned to the hospital about 10 a.m. wishing to take the child home whether or not he had appendicitis but were persuaded to wait till midday when he was seen by the consultant surgeon. At this examination nothing abnormal was found except a slightly raised pulse rate and the child was therefore discharged home as the parents wished, but it seemed that none of the doctors concerned thought to warn them that the possibility of appendicitis could not be entirely excluded or that medical supervision should be continued.

Shortly after arriving home the child seemed much worse, and another surgeon diagnosed a perforated appendix which was confirmed at operation the same evening in the private block of another hospital. A great deal of pus was found but improvement was rapid after intravenous tetracycline was started on the second postoperative day. He was discharged on the eighth day but readmitted on the following day for six days with a pelvic abscess which required draining; after this he made an excellent recovery.

In due course the father instructed solicitors to write to the hospital claiming damages and alleging negligence of the doctors in failing to diagnose acute appendicitis. It was considered that the omission to give the warning referred to above would make difficult a successful defence in court and the claim was finally settled on an *ex gratia* basis, without admission of liability, by the protection society paying the hospital's charges and surgeons' fees plus solicitors' costs.

On 2nd September 1960 an eleven-year-old boy injured his left arm in a fall and was taken to the casualty department of the local hospital, where he was found to have fractures of the lower ends of the radius and ulna. Displacement was severe, and the fractures were reduced by the senior casualty officer under general anaesthesia. A plaster slab was applied and his mother was told to bring him back the next day, and again a week later on 10th September. When he attended the next morning as instructed he was seen by a recently qualified house surgeon. She considered the splint was loose and therefore told the sister in charge to apply a crepe bandage. Although in the vicinity, she did not actually watch the bandaging but was satisfied with the result before sending the boy home with specific directions to keep the fingers moving. On this occasion no adult accompanied the boy. Neither then nor previously were any written instructions given regarding his next attendance. He was therefore not due to attend again until 10th September but he returned on the evening of the 6th with his hand blue and swollen and complaining of pain at the elbow and wrist. He was seen again by the house surgeon who removed the plaster slab and ordered its replacement by a totally encircling well-padded plaster to include the elbow joint. Before the boy left, the doctor split the plaster and spent some time telling his sister that he must attend again on the morrow.

When he failed to arrive as ordered, the house surgeon told the casualty officer about her anxiety but did nothing further. On 8th September the child came to hospital obviously very ill and in great pain and his hand was found to be black, with the skin blistered. The senior casualty officer immediately ordered his transfer to another hospital where a surgeon found it necessary to amputate the arm above the elbow as the limb was gangrenous up to this joint.

Within six weeks of his last attendance at the first hospital, a claim was lodged on his behalf against the hospital board and the statement of claim presented was most formidable, claiming damages of nearly £18,000 including special damages amounting to £2,800.

When the case was reported to the protection society it was agreed that no liability should be accepted on the part of the house surgeon mainly because the hospital administration appeared to be at fault in allowing such an inexperienced young doctor to assume responsibilities for which she was quite untrained. This opinion was conveyed to the hospital's insurers who replied pointing out that despite the member's acknowledged inexperience, her failure to make sure on 3rd September that the crepe bandage was not applied too tightly and her failure to consult a senior colleague before ordering the replacement of the plaster slab on 6th September could not be ignored.

Shortly before the trial the protection society was formally invited to contribute to a settlement and agreement was reached for a contribution of 20 per cent of the sum negotiated.

Early in 1961 a radiologist in New Zealand undertook to perform an aortogram as an essential preliminary to surgical treatment on a patient suffering from a thoracic aneurysm. His procedure (the Seldinger technique) was as follows: He first inserted into the femoral artery a trocar and cannula through which was slipped a plastic catheter which with the guide wire, was passed upwards through the common iliac artery into the aorta, but at this stage further progress proved impossible and with further attempts obstruction occurred at successively lower levels. The investigation was therefore abandoned and the patient returned to the ward. Within an hour pain developed in the upper thigh; this was diagnosed as due to a femoral thrombosis but embolectomy proved unsuccessful owing to the tortuous and grossly atheromatous state of the vessel. Despite every effort by medical treatment to restore circulation in the leg, it had to be amputated after four days. Healing of the stump was slow and complicated by sepsis and the development of infective hepatitis. Fourteen months after the operation, solicitors notified the hospital of a claim. The statement of claim contained three main allegations: firstly, that the radiologist caused the femoral thrombosis by his unskilful investigation; secondly, that the surgeon failed to diagnose the condition and treat it promptly; and thirdly, that a blood transfusion the patient had received was the origin of an homologous serum jaundice which he developed during his convalescence.

The trial of the action was deferred for various reasons but mainly because certain key witnesses were travelling abroad at different times. During this period several efforts were made on behalf of the plaintiff to induce the defendant to settle the case by an *ex gratia* payment rather than contest it. All these overtures were firmly rejected but in June 1962 an amended statement of claim was submitted which included the allegation in respect of the aortogram that the patient was informed by one of the doctors that 'there was no risk whatever attached to this minor operation' and it was claimed that if he had been properly informed of the risk, he would not have consented to the investigation. The case finally came to trial in April 1963, and the following questions were put to the jury and answered in the way indicated: '1. Was the defendant by its servants or agents negligent so as to involve the plaintiff in the loss of his leg in (*a*) embarking upon an investigation by aortogram? Answer: No; (*b*) using a catheter in an unskilful manner? Answer: No; (*c*) failing to inform the plaintiff adequately of the risks of conducting a formal aortogram upon him? Answer: Yes. 2. Did the plaintiff contract jaundice as a result of negligence on the part of the defendant by its servants or agents? Answer: No.'

General damages were assessed at £3,000 and special damages at £2,651. 10s. 11d., but the judge granted a stay of execution so that the defendants could consider filing a motion for judgment or for a new trial despite the jury's verdict. The society approved the filing of the motion and further agreed that if these proceedings were unsuccessful the case should be taken to appeal. The hearing of the motion took place in June 1963 and in November judgment was delivered in favour of the defendant. The written judgment was a closely reasoned, comprehensive, and erudite document of some 28 foolscap pages. Briefly, the Judge's opinion was that where some special investigation was an essential preliminary to life-saving surgery (as in this case) the relatively remote but inevitable risk of such an investigation must be accepted in the overall interest of the patient. In this case he considered the doctors concerned were justified in not mentioning the specific hazards of the procedure to the patient as this would have served no useful purpose but would have caused unnecessary alarm and distress; their decision was reasonable and made in good faith.

A patient attended the out-patient department of a hospital in New Zealand with a laceration of his left forearm involving the muscle; he was seen by the house surgeon who sutured the wound. When seen a few days later the wound was healing satisfactorily and he was able to return to light duties in a little over two weeks.

About one month after the original injury the casualty officer was asked by a sister to examine the patient again as he had returned with signs of infection and lymphangitis. This request was made as the casualty officer was passing by to suture the wounds of an accident case and he made the remark that the patient would probably need penicillin. After completing the suturing he returned to see the patient and found that the sister had already given the penicillin although it was discovered that the patient's card was marked in red ink 'sensitive to penicillin'. Fortunately, in spite of this alleged sensitivity there was very little allergic reaction, but subsequently two 'flare-ups' occurred which, however, settled quickly.

A claim was initiated on behalf of the patient against the casualty officer, but while he himself felt that he had overall responsibility for the error that had occurred in the department, it was considered that a clear duty also lay upon the sister to have regard to the entry on the patient's record card which was available to her, and to this extent a contribution from the hospital's insurers seemed reasonable. A small sum was eventually accepted by the patient, to which the hospital insurers contributed 50 per cent.

A woman of thirty-four became pregnant for the first time after several years of married life. During the course of her antenatal surveillance her blood was found to be Rh-negative and to have a high antibody titre, while her husband was Rh-positive. The antibody titre was so high that investigations were made and revealed that a year or so previously she had received a transfusion of Rh-positive blood. As a result of this she was watched most carefully, and induction of labour was attempted at the 37th week but was unsuccessful and Caesarean section was therefore performed. The baby suffered from haemolytic disease and received an exchange transfusion. The subsequent progress of both mother and child was extremely satisfactory.

Investigation showed that some time earlier the patient had been involved in a road accident and taken to hospital where, after her blood was grouped and found to be Group A, Rh-negative, she was given two pints of blood after cross-matching. Shortly afterwards, however, she was transferred to another hospital where a further transfusion was given, this time consisting of three pints of 'A positive' blood. No reaction was recorded and the mistake was not discovered until the antenatal investigations. It appeared that this blood had been cross-matched in the laboratory where the record book showed her blood as being of Group A, Rh-positive. It seems that after her transfer the doctor concerned with her care in the ward had correctly entered in the case sheets the information that she was Group A, but erroneously added that she was Rh-positive. At this hospital it seemed that while those patients whose blood group was unknown were grouped in the normal way, those whose group was thought to be already established were not re-grouped on admission, reliance being placed on what were thought to be previous findings. Thus, the only check in such a case as this would be the cross-matching of the blood before transfusion, and this did not reveal the incompatibility.

It had to be admitted that the need for the Caesarean section was directly related to the fact that the patient had been Rh-immunised by the transfusion, and although the operation went well in all respects and the infant was quite normal the patient's capacity to have further trouble-free pregnancies had been prejudiced. It seemed fair that the responsibility should be shared between the doctor who was in charge of the haematological and transfusion services, and the hospital authorities, and it was agreed that a 50 per cent contribution to a settlement should be made by each.

The question of quantum produced very serious difficulties as it was almost impossible to assess fairly the damage suffered, and then to translate this into monetary terms. After considerable negotiation a settlement was agreed.

A young man slipped on a wet road and stubbed the middle finger of his right hand. He went to the casualty department of the local hospital where he was seen by the casualty officer. X-ray examination of the hand revealed a fracture of the middle phalanx, and the casualty officer instructed a nurse to apply a collodion splint. This was done forthwith and inspected by the doctor shortly afterwards. He decided it was firm enough for the patient to leave.

Just outside the hospital building the patient lit a cigarette and was horrified to see his recently applied dressing burst into flames. He rushed back to the casualty department where the first-degree burns he sustained on his index finger and thumb were appropriately treated. The burns were fully healed in two months without any residual scarring. The patient had not been warned of the inflammable nature of the collodion and his subsequent claim for damages could not be resisted.

6. Statutes Relating to Negligence

Negligence has its roots – and they are comparatively speaking shallow roots – in the common law deriving from actions on the Case. Much of the law of negligence is judge-made, and the preceding chapters have, it is hoped, given some indication of the manner in which judges have set about their tasks and demonstrated that which weighed with them in coming to their judgments. This chapter will deal with the third type of law – statute law – and set out the principal Acts of Parliament that establish the framework within which the Judiciary act when allegations of negligence come before them.

Fatal Accidents Acts, 1846–1959

Prior to the introduction, in 1846, of Lord Campbell's Act the position was as stated in *Baker* v. *Bolton:*[1] 'In a civil court the death of a human being could not be complained of as an injury.' The Fatal Accidents Acts have, where death has been caused by the wrongful act of another, allowed near relatives who were dependant on the deceased to claim compensation in respect of pecuniary loss, actual or prospective, but not speculative. The onus is upon the plaintiffs, the personal representatives, to prove the loss and there is no claim in respect of wounded feelings or natural grief. Where there is also a gain resulting from the death this will normally be taken into consideration, but the 1959 Act specifically excludes account being taken of 'any insurance money, benefit (national insurance) pension or gratuity' which arises from death.

A case of medical interest in connection with these Acts was that of *Pigney* v. *Pointer's Transport Service*[2] where, following a head injury, anxiety neurosis and depression developed and the deceased committed suicide. The dependant's claim was held not to be barred by the fact of suicide.

1. (1808) 1 Camp 493. 2. (1957) 1 WLR 1121.

The Partnership Act, 1890

The need for ensuring that one's partners maintain adequate cover is shown by this extract from the Act: 'Where for any wrongful act or omission of any partner acting in the ordinary course of the business of the firm or with the authority of his co-partners loss or injury is caused to any person not being a partner in the firm . . . the firm is liable therefore to the same extent as the partner so acting or omitting to act.'

Supreme Court of Judicature (Consolidation) Act, 1925
Supreme Court of Judicature (Amendment) Act, 1959

By these Acts the High Court can, on application by the Attorney General, decree that a person be prohibited from commencing or continuing proceedings without leave of the High Court or of one of the Judges of that Court. Doctors have a particular liability to become the target of the unreasonable litigant, as the following case will illustrate.

A consultant psychiatrist was requested by the Procurator Fiscal to examine and report upon a prisoner who had been charged with two breaches of the peace. The psychiatrist submitted a comprehensive report which included a detailed description of his interview with the offender; this supported vividly a diagnosis of paranoia with lack of insight, and he offered his opinion that the man was certifiable as insane and unfit to plead.

On the basis of this report and other medical testimony the prisoner was ultimately transferred to a mental hospital but not before the question of his sanity had been dealt with in open court in proceedings conducted by himself which lasted nine days.

From the hospital to which he was admitted the patient soon escaped, remained at liberty for twenty-eight days and then returned to his home town. Without benefit of legal advice, he immediately embarked on a spate of further litigation and later succeeded in getting himself elected as local Councillor. His activities culminated in the issue of a writ against fourteen individuals including prominent local businessmen, lawyers and doctors, with the psychiatrist among those cited. The writ named the Defenders and continued, 'who are hereby charged by the Pursuer as having all joined and been concerned in the common illegal purposes of a conspiracy of vexatious litigations, Abduction, Defamation and trafficking in concocted and calumnous Divorce, and Custody Orders, conducted against him, and to alienate and loot under colour of law the dwellinghouse at . . . . . Road, ...'. The Pursuer referred to his action as one of 'Restitution redress, damages and of ejection and Delivery' and included with the writ a statement of claim running to forty-nine foolscap pages.

When the psychiatrist forwarded these documents to the society he wrote that although 'I have not yet completely despaired . . . of the small voice of commonsense eventually breaking through to find some legally acceptable way of dealing with this man, I can see at present no end to his litigation, which goes from Sheriff Court to Court of Session and even to Appeal and back again'.

When the case before the Lower Court was dismissed the Pursuer appealed to the Court of Session which, after one abortive hearing, finally rejected the appeal but did not find it necessary to give reasons.

However, the end was in sight, for shortly after this the society's solicitors' agents advised that the Lord Advocate (the Scottish equivalent of Attorney General) had instructed proceedings in the Supreme Court to have this man prohibited from serving future actions in the Scottish Court.

Law Reform (Miscellaneous Provisions) Act, 1934

The common law rule was that the death of the plaintiff or defendant extinguished rights of action in tort – the legal maxim being *actio personalis moritur cum persona.* The Law Reform (Miscellaneous Provisions) Act provided that, with certain exceptions which need not concern us here, 'On the death of any person . . . all causes of action subsisting against or vested in him shall survive against, or, as the case may be, for the benefit of his estate'.

Certain rules relate to the damages that may be awarded. First, damages recoverable for the benefit of the estate of a deceased person, i.e. where the personal representatives prosecute the claim, may not include exemplary damages. Second, where the death has been caused by the act or omission which gives rise to the action, the damages shall be calculated without reference to any loss or gain to the estate due to the death except that a sum in respect of funeral expenses may be included.

Proceedings are only maintainable where they were pending at the time of the defendant's death or are begun not later than six months after his personal representatives took out representation.

The problem of a person dying before or at the same time as his act or omission caused damage to another is dealt with by a provision that such a case shall be treated as though the cause of action existed before his death

Law Reform (Married Women and Tortfeasors) Act, 1935

The position under common law was that where a joint tort had been committed the plaintiff could choose his victim and could recover against him in full, the defendant having no claim against any other tortfeasor for a proportion of the damages.

The Law Reform (Married Women and Tortfeasors) Act provides that, 'Where damage is suffered by any person as a result of a tort . . . any tortfeasor liable in respect of that damage may recover contribution from any other tortfeasor who is or would if sued have been liable in respect of the same damage whether as a joint tortfeasor or otherwise . . .'. The implication of the phrase 'as a joint tortfeasor or otherwise' is that contributions may be sought where two separate torts lead to the same damage and not only where two or more persons are concerned together in a joint tort.

Limitation Act, 1939

Law Reform (Limitation of Actions, Etc.) Act, 1954

Limitation Act, 1963

The 1939 Act provided that action founded on tort should not be brought after the expiration of six years from the date on which the cause of action occurred. Extensions were available, however, where the plaintiff was under the disability of infancy or unsoundness of mind or where there had been fraud or mistake.

Where a person having a right of action is an infant or of unsound mind the statute does not begin to run until either the disability is at an end or the person dies.

Where the action is based upon fraud or the right of action is concealed by fraud or the action is for relief from the consequences of a mistake, the period of limitation does not begin to run until the plaintiff has discovered the fraud or mistake or could with reasonable diligence have done so.

The Law Reform (Limitation of Actions, Etc.) Act 1954 reduced the limitation period in the case of actions arising from personal injuries caused by negligence, nuisance or breach of duty, to three years. A similar period was also enacted for actions under the Fatal Accidents Acts.

The Limitation Act 1963 which applies to personal injuries arising from negligence, nuisance or breach of duty, makes provision for cases such as that of *Cartledge* v. *E. Jobling & Sons Ltd,*[3] where miners, being unaware of the harm they had suffered, were left without a remedy. It enacts that, with the leave of the court, an action may be started within a year of the time when the plaintiff discovered or ought to have discovered his cause of action notwithstanding that the normal three years period had by that time expired.

Law Reform (Contributory Negligence) Act 1945

Section 1 of this Act reads,with a clarity as commendable as it is unusual, as follows: 'Where any person suffers damage as the result partly of his own fault and partly of the fault of any other person or persons a claim in respect of that damage shall not be defeated by reason of the fault of the person suffering the damage but the damages recoverable in respect thereof shall be reduced to such extent as the court thinks just and equitable having regard to the claimant's share in the responsibility for the damage . . .' This Act put an end to the previous very unsatisfactory state of affairs whereby if a person's own negligence had contributed to the loss and damage he forfeited all claims in respect of that loss and damage.

Law Reform (Personal Injuries) Act, 1948

This act provided that in assessing any loss of earnings or profits resulting from the injuries complained of account should be taken of one half of the estimated benefits from national insurance sources. Further it provided that in considering medical expenses claimed, the fact that treatment could have been obtained under the National Health Service should be disregarded.

Legal Aid Acts, 1949 – 1964

The 1949 Act made it possible for persons with limited financial means to obtain legal advice and assistance in pursuing claims they would otherwise have been quite unable to undertake. The assisted litigant is assessed as to what contribution, if any, he should make,

3. (1963) 1 A11 ER 341 (1963) AC 758.

the balance of the costs coming from the legal aid fund. This Act left those persons who had successfully defended themselves against legally aided litigants without any means of obtaining reimbursement of the costs incurred.

The 1964 Act provided that following a successful defence against a legally aided plaintiff the defendant could obtain payment of his costs from the legal aid fund where the court thought it just and equitable and where he would otherwise suffer 'severe financial hardship'.

7. The Future of Medical Negligence

Medical negligence is concerned very largely with personal injuries, and it is proposed to confine this short chapter to a discussion of possible developments in this field. Personal injury can, of course, result from many types of negligence other than medical or from causes quite distinct from negligence. Where a person is injured the question of whether he receives compensation, apart from National Insurance or personal accident insurance benefits, depends upon whether or not he can prove negligence against some other person or persons. This is logical enough, but logic aside there is a natural human feeling that the injured should be compensated. Frequently, a doctor reporting a mishap in which a patient has suffered harm will say that while he entirely refutes any suggestion of negligence, nevertheless he hopes that his patient will receive compensation. This feeling, it is thought, may prove in the long run to be a decisive factor.

The original concept of negligence was based on the wrongdoer making direct compensation to his victim. Under modern conditions this has ceased to be a practical proposition and those who are liable to find themselves defending an allegation of negligence insure against this risk wherever possible. The extent to which the emphasis is today on compensation rather than on blameworthiness is shown by the Employers' (Defective Equipment) Act 1969 which provides that where an employee suffers personal injury due to defective equipment, the fault being that of a third party, the employer shall be held liable in negligence.

And is blameworthiness so important? Any plaintiff would prefer the defendant to be defiant but insured rather than contrite but insolvent. The subscribers to the Medical Protection Society do so for their own protection but also to ensure that should their patient suffer from their negligence, the wherewithal for compensation is available. Protection organisations are pro-doctor but in no way anti-patient.

The attitude of the court to blameworthiness is far from clear. Lord Justice Denning in the case of *Hatcher* v. *Black*[1] said, 'You should only only find him guilty of negligence when he falls short of the standard of a reasonably skilful medical man. In short, when he is deserving of censure – for negligence in a medical man is deserving of censure.' In the case referred to on pages 53–55, however, the Judge said, 'I wish to emphasise that no moral blame attaches to him' – no hint of censure here.

It may be that judges differ between themselves as to whether matters of censure, moral rather than legal issues, are for them to pronounce upon. To say, without qualification, that negligence in a medical man is deserving of censure is surely far too sweeping a statement. Every professional man has at some time in his career been negligent, and every professional man, with the remarkable exception of the barrister, has therefore been at risk of finding himself sued in negligence. In the vast majority of cases, however, there has been ample reason, illness, overwork, tiredness, worry, misunderstanding, and so on, and the attitude of professional colleagues is almost without exception one of sympathy, not of censure.

If, then, the moral issue of blameworthiness does not run parallel with the legal issue of negligence, is there any virtue in retaining the latter? Does the law of negligence as at present administered fulfil the reasonable needs of the plaintiff who has suffered personal injury, and does it deal fairly with the defendant? The defects are evident. It may be a matter of years after the event before the case comes to court and the reliability of evidence given after such an interval must often be suspect. The plaintiff may be in financial difficulty for a prolonged period after his injury when he is least able to earn. If successful, he is awarded a lump sum which is assessed, having regard to his expectation of life and his earnings prior to his injury. Such assessment may, in the event, prove to have been unduly generous if he be short-lived, or totally inadequate should the opposite apply. The legal costs may be disproportionate to the value of the case and may, especially in the case of legally aided litigants, lead to settlements that bear little relation to the merits of the case.

Some of these difficulties might be surmounted by an early hearing of the issue of liability, leaving that of quantum to be

1. (1954) C.L.Y.2289. *The Times*, 2nd July.

determined at a later date should the plaintiff be successful on the primary issue. Instalment payments as necessary might also be ordered. This would certainly result in the plaintiff receiving some early relief, but it would also give him a vested interest in maintaining his disability, and the unsuccessful defendant would be faced with an open-ended liability.

What merits are there to set against these objections? Retribution cannot be one. Cases are, in general, only fought where there is a reasonable defence, so blameworthiness, if any, cannot be great. Insurance takes care of the financial side, and the main punishment for the unsuccessful defendant is the danger of adverse publicity, a fickle jade dependent on many extraneous factors but quite unrelated to the degree of negligence. It might be thought that negligence cases reported in the Press have a helpful effect in both warning and instructing others. This may have validity in some fields but not, it is thought, in medical negligence. The doctor who has operated on the wrong side does not need a judge to tell him how to avoid a repetition of such an incident, and the protection organisations do their utmost to instruct practitioners and students in the hazards of modern medicine and surgery. So unpredictable indeed are the results of negligence actions that one recalls the words of an Irish judge who said that, compared with litigation, horse-racing was an exact science!

Is litigation in fact appropriate in cases of personal injury? Is it in accordance with present-day thought that if two persons suffer the same injury they should receive quite disproportionate compensation dependent upon whether or not negligence can be proved. Might then civil negligence, so far as personal injury is concerned, be abolished and a method be evolved which would secure early and adequate compensation for the victim and leave any wrongdoer to be dealt with by the criminal law, his employer, and his peers as the facts might require?

Whether any such scheme should be based on private insurance or included under National Insurance is perhaps a political question, and the compromise might be a basis of National Insurance with an addition of private for those who so desired. The virtue of any such scheme would be that the injured person would only have to prove personal injury and not negligence and payment could be on a monthly or quarterly basis with medical reviews of the disability from time to time as required.

Where medical negligence is concerned, the essential difficulty would be to distinguish between an injury that occurred while the patient was under investigation or treatment, and a natural complication of the original condition. Problems would certainly arise in borderline cases, but experience and precedent would quickly provide working guidelines.

Would patients take kindly to the thought of insuring against possible injury while in hospital? As science replaces mystique in medicine, it is thought that a sizeable proportion of the population is sufficiently adult to appreciate that the complexities of modern medicine must inevitably entail risks – and it is, of course, the patient who takes the risk. There is surely no essential difference between insuring against the risks in hospital and insuring against the risks involved in a journey by air or rail. Indeed, were the necessary facilities easily available, many might today be prepared to purchase units of insurance on admission to hospital and to forgo any rights they might have in negligence for the assurance of prompt payments of a pre-selected sum during any extra period of incapacity caused by the injury.

Would any such developments lead to a lessening of the standard of care? It is suggested that, if anything, the reverse would be the case. Doctors would be freed from the anxiety of negligence actions and there would be no temptation to make less than full disclosure to the patient of any mishap that might occur. If and when such a mishap took place, it would often prove possible for the doctor to continue caring for his patient and it would often be in the patient's interests that he should do so. As things are, the solicitor's letter alleging negligence is usually heralded or followed by a change of practitioner; a change which may be far from beneficial. Indeed, the patient is often the one who is complaining the least – his advisers, however, refer him elsewhere, or a doctor feels that he cannot continue in view of the allegations made. Adequate insurance could bring understanding on the patient's part and sympathy and extra care on the doctor's, which together would provide a very different atmosphere from that engendered by impending litigation. One needs no deep psychological insight to appreciate in which environment the patient's injuries are most likely to improve.

8. The Avoidance of Negligence

The following pointers, while in no way exhaustive, could, it is thought, lead to a welcome reduction in the number of allegations of negligence being brought against doctors.

1. Time spent securing and maintaining rapport with one's patient is not time wasted – many allegations of negligence are preceded by a breakdown in personal relationships.
2. An inadequate history leads to an inadequate diagnosis and inadequate treatment.
3. The history taken by one's colleague may or may not have been complete.
4. If the patient does not progress as expected, re-examine – and re-take the history.
5. It can be difficult to defend a failure to X-ray or to make use of ancillary methods of investigation.
6. The scaphoid has more negligence actions to its discredit than any other bone
7. Glass foreign bodies are commonly missed – and most glass is radio-opaque.
8. Missed intra-ocular foreign bodies are becoming increasingly common
9. Beware the double injury in the one limb – if the joint cannot be moved through its full range it must be X-rayed.
10. An X-ray of an injured limb should include the joint above and below.
11. A second opinion is a safeguard for the patient – and for the doctor.
12. The professional man is expected to maintain his standard of professional knowledge and skill.
13. Save in emergency, it is dangerous to go outside one's specialty or treat beyond one's competence.

14. Many complainents allege that another doctor expressed or implied criticism. Such criticism is almost invariably unfair, as the second doctor is seldom viewing the case from the same position as was the first.
15. The law does not require a doctor to guarantee results; care should be taken to see that the patient has no grounds for considering that a guarantee has been implied. Currently, this is of particular importance in vasectomy.
16. Notes, adequate, legible and signed, are the doctor's main defence.
17. Copies of letters should be retained.
18. Being liable for the negligence of one's employees, one must be satisfied regarding their training, qualifications, and competence.
19. Misunderstandings regarding fees can lead to allegations of negligence when attempts are made to collect.
20. Prescribing drugs with which one is unfamiliar is an unnecessary hazard.
21. Equipment needs understanding and regular maintenance.
22. When patients are told of a deputy, the deputy should be told of the patients.
23. The knowledge that a doctor is insured encourages a certain type of patient to lodge a claim.
24. One cannot be judge in one's own case; liability should therefore never be admitted.

Index to Statutes

Index to Cases

General Index